Maximise your memory with CGP!

This amazing CGP Knowledge Organiser will help you remember all the key concepts for KS3 Maths! It's ideal if you're working at foundation level.

We've condensed every topic down to the essentials, with step-by-step methods and worked examples — much quicker than doing it yourself!

And to see if it's all sunk in, there's also a matching Knowledge Retriever book. It'll test your memory of every single page!

CGP — still the best! ☺

Our sole aim here at CGP is to produce the highest quality books — carefully written, immaculately presented and dangerously close to being funny.

Then we work our socks off to get them out to you
— at the cheapest possible prices.

Contents

Section 1 — Numbers

Calculating Tips 2
More Calculating Tips 3
Place Value and Ordering Numbers 4
Addition and Subtraction 5
Multiplying and Dividing
   by 10, 100, etc. 6
Multiplying without a Calculator 7
Dividing without a Calculator 8
Special Types of Number 9
Prime Numbers,
   Multiples and Factors 10
Prime Factors, LCM and HCF 11
Fractions, Decimals
   and Percentages 12
Fractions 13
Fraction Calculations 14
Percentages 15
Rounding Numbers 16
Rounding and Estimation 17
Powers and Roots 18

Section 2 — Algebra and Graphs

Algebra Basics 19
Formulas 20
Solving Equations 21
Number Patterns and Sequences 22
Coordinates and
   Straight-Line Graphs 23
Straight-Line Graphs 24
Straight-Line Graphs and Plotting 25
Reading Off Graphs 26
Travel and Conversion Graphs 27

Section 3 — Ratio, Proportion and Rates of Change

Ratios and Proportion 28
Proportion Problems 29
Percentage Increase and Decrease 30
Units and Conversions 31
Reading Timetables 32
Maps and Map Scales 33
Scale Drawings 34
Speed 35

Section 4 — Geometry and Measures

Symmetry and Regular Polygons	36
Triangles and Quadrilaterals	37
Congruence and Similarity	38
Perimeter and Area	39
Area and Compound Area	40
Circles	41
3D Shapes	42
Nets and Surface Area	43
Volume	44
Angle Basics	45
Measuring and Drawing Angles	46
Geometry Rules	47
Parallel Lines	48
Interior and Exterior Angles	49
Translation and Reflection	50
Rotation and Enlargement	51
Triangle Construction	52
Constructions	53

Section 5 — Probability and Statistics

Probability	54
Listing Outcomes	55
Venn Diagrams	56
Types of Data and Line Graphs	57
Pictograms and Bar Charts	58
Pie Charts	59
Mean, Median, Mode and Range	60
Frequency Tables	61
Scatter Graphs	62

Published by CGP.
Written by Richard Parsons.

Editors: Sarah George, Rob Hayman, Samuel Mann, Caley Simpson.

With thanks to Alastair Duncombe and David Ryan for the proofreading.
With thanks to Jan Greenway for the copyright research.

ISBN: 978 1 78908 859 5

Printed by Elanders Ltd, Newcastle upon Tyne.
Clipart from Corel®

Text, design, layout and original illustrations © Richard Parsons 2021
All rights reserved.

Photocopying more than one section of this book is not permitted, even if you have a CLA licence.
Extra copies are available from CGP with next day delivery. • 0800 1712 712 • www.cgpbooks.co.uk

Section 1 — Numbers

Calculating Tips

Three Steps for Wordy Questions

1. **Underline** the information needed to answer the question.
2. Write the question in **maths**.
3. **Work out** the answer — show your working clearly.

EXAMPLE

1. Iain uses a code to save <u>25%</u> on his online shopping. It should cost <u>£10</u>. How much money does he <u>save</u>?

2. 25% of £10
   = 0.25 × 10
   = £2.50 3

You can do the calculation without units — but always add them back in for the final answer.

BODMAS

BODMAS gives the order of operations:

1. **B**rackets
2. **O**ther
3. **D**ivision and **M**ultiplication
4. **A**ddition and **S**ubtraction

'Other' is things like squaring or cubing.

Work left to right when there's **only** division and multiplication OR **only** addition and subtraction.

EXAMPLE

Work out:

a) $(4 - 2)^2 \times 3$

$(4 - 2)^2 \times 3 = 2^2 \times 3$ 1
$= 4 \times 3$ 2
$= 12$ 3

You won't always need to use all the steps.

b) $5 \times (9 - 6) - 7 + 10$

$5 \times (9 - 6) - 7 + 10$
$= 5 \times 3 - 7 + 10$ 1
$= 15 - 7 + 10$ 3
$= 8 + 10 = 18$ 4

Hidden Brackets in Fractions

For a fraction with calculations on top and bottom:

1. Put top and bottom in **brackets**.
2. Work out top and bottom.
3. **Divide** the results.

EXAMPLE

Calculate $\dfrac{100 \div 2 + 10}{3 \times 4}$

1. $\dfrac{(100 \div 2 + 10)}{(3 \times 4)}$

2. $= \dfrac{(50 + 10)}{(3 \times 4)} = \dfrac{60}{12} = 5$ 3

Follow BODMAS to work out the answer — brackets come first.

More Calculating Tips

Opposite Operations

Addition is the opposite of subtraction: 20 + 17 = 37   ⟷   37 − 17 = 20

Multiplication is the opposite of division: 9 × 5 = 45   ⟷   45 ÷ 5 = 9

Use opposite operations to check an answer:

1. Do the opposite operation to your answer.
2. Check it's the number you started with.

EXAMPLE

Edwina has 8 boxes containing 6 eggs each. She works out she has 48 eggs in total. Is she correct?

1. 48 ÷ 6 = 8 boxes
2. This is the number of boxes Edwina has, so she is correct.

Patterns in Calculations

Use opposite operations to make numbers in calculations easier to work with.

If you add to one number, subtract same amount from the other:

+5 ⤵ 95 + 105 ⤴ −5   = 200
    100 + 100   = 200

If you multiply one number, divide the other by same amount:

×2 ⤵ 21 × 8 ⤴ ÷2   = 168
     42 × 4   = 168
×2 ⤵ 84 × 2 ⤴ ÷2   = 168

Calculators

Shift (2nd function) — press to use what's written above other buttons

Fractions — used to input and simplify fractions, and to swap between fractions/decimals

Memory — used to store and recall answers to use in later calculations

The ANSWER

Square, cube and root buttons

Brackets — calculators use BODMAS, so make sure to include brackets

π — the number 'pi' (3.141...), used in circle calculations

ANS — recalls the last answer calculated

Section 1 — Numbers

Place Value and Ordering Numbers

Place Value in Whole Numbers

The digits are the values (0-9) in each column.

Millions	Hundred-thousands	Ten-thousands	Thousands	Hundreds	Tens	Units
6	3	8	5	2	7	4

Starting from the right and moving left, put a space between every three digits: 6 385 274

Read each group of three digits as a separate number: six million, three hundred and eighty-five thousand, two hundred and seventy-four

Plaice value

Ordering Numbers

1. Sort into groups by number of digits.
2. Put each group in size order.

EXAMPLE

Put these numbers in order from smallest to largest:
3801 7 675 1238 25 219 5 83

1-digit	2-digits	3-digits	4-digits
7 5	25 83	675 219	3801 1238

② 5 7 25 83 219 675 1238 3801

Place Value in Decimals

Hundreds	Tens	Units	Decimal point	Tenths	Hundredths	Thousandths
2	1	9	.	3	6	5

Read digits after the decimal point as separate numbers: two hundred and nineteen point three six five

Ordering Decimals

1. Order by whole number part.
2. Put decimal parts in order by comparing the digits in each decimal place working from left to right.

EXAMPLE

Put these numbers in order from smallest to largest:
1.9 0.2 0.045 3.7 0.009 0.07 2.46

① 0.2 0.045 0.009 0.07 | 1.9 | 2.46 | 3.7

② 0.009 0.045 0.07 0.2 1.9 2.46 3.7

For numbers between 0 and 1, the more zeros after the decimal point, the smaller they are — so 0.01 is smaller than 0.1.

Section 1 — Numbers

Addition and Subtraction

Adding Whole Numbers

1. **Line up** units columns.
2. **Add up** columns from right to left.
3. **Carry over** any spare tens to next column.

EXAMPLE

Work out 634 + 275 + 43

① 634
   275
+ 43

② 634
   275
+ 43
      2
    1

③ 634
   275
+ 43
    52
  1 1

634
275
+ 43
952
1 1

Adding Decimals

1. **Line up** decimal points.
2. **Write in extra zeros** so decimals are same length.
3. **Add up** columns as above.

EXAMPLE

Calculate 4.98 + 3.5

① 4.98
+ 3.50

② 4.98
+ 3.50

③ 4.98
+ 3.50
     8

4.98
+ 3.50
  .48
   1

4.98
+ 3.50
8.48
  1

Put a decimal point in the answer line too.

Subtracting Whole Numbers

1. **Line up** units columns.
2. **Subtract** bottom number from top number, working right to left.
3. **Borrow 10** from the column to the left if top number is smaller than bottom number.

EXAMPLE

Subtract 129 from 863

① 863
− 129

② 8⁵6̸¹3
− 129
    4

③ 9 is bigger than 3, so borrow 10 from next column.

8⁵6̸¹3
− 129
  34

8⁵6̸¹3
− 129
734

Subtracting Decimals

1. **Line up** decimal points.

If a question involves money, change amounts to £ to get decimal values.

2. **Write in extra zeros** so decimals are same length.
3. **Subtract** columns as above.

EXAMPLE

Ezra has £4 and spends 73p. How much does he have left?

① £4.00
− £0.73

② There's nothing to borrow here, so borrow from the next column.
Now you can borrow 10.

③ £⁴3̸.¹00
− £0.73

£⁴3̸.⁹¹0̸0
− £0.73
     . 7

£⁴3̸.⁹¹0̸0
− £0.73
£3.27

Section 1 — Numbers

Multiplying and Dividing by 10, 100, etc.

Multiplying by 10, 100, etc.

① Count the number of zeros.
② Move the decimal point that many places BIGGER (⌣).
③ Add zeros before decimal point if needed.

EXAMPLE

a) 24 × 10
① × 10 has 1 zero
② d.p. moves 1 place
③ So 24 × 10 = 240

b) 8.7 × 100
① × 100 has 2 zeros
② d.p. moves 2 places
③ So 8.7 × 100 = 870

c) 0.95 × 1000
① × 1000 has 3 zeros
② d.p. moves 3 places
③ So 0.95 × 1000 = 950

Dividing by 10, 100, etc.

① Count the number of zeros.
② Move the decimal point that many places SMALLER (⌢).
③ Add or remove zeros if needed.

EXAMPLE

a) 160 ÷ 10
① ÷ 10 has 1 zero
② d.p. moves 1 place
③ So 160 ÷ 10 = 16

b) 385 ÷ 100
① ÷ 100 has 2 zeros
② d.p. moves 2 places
So 385 ÷ 100 = 3.85

c) 29.3 ÷ 1000
① ÷ 1000 has 3 zeros
② d.p. moves 3 places
③ So 29.3 ÷ 1000 = 0.0293

Multiplying and Dividing by Multiples of 10, 100, etc.

① Multiply/divide by 1st digit of the number.
② Count the number of zeros.
③ Move the decimal point that many places BIGGER or SMALLER.
④ Add or remove zeros if needed.

EXAMPLE

Calculate 12 × 600
① 12 × 6 = 72
② × 100 has 2 zeros
③ d.p. moves 2 places bigger
④ 72 × 100 = 7200

The calculation is split into 12 × 6 × 100.

EXAMPLE

Calculate 36 ÷ 4000
① 36 ÷ 4 = 9
② ÷ 1000 has 3 zeros
③ d.p. moves 3 places smaller
④ 9 ÷ 1000 = 0.009

Section 1 — Numbers

Multiplying without a Calculator

Traditional Method

1. **Line up** numbers in columns.
2. **Split** into **two** multiplications.
3. **Add up** results from right to left.

EXAMPLE

Work out 49 × 34.

①   4 9
       × 3 4

② 4 × 49 = 196 → 1 9$_3$ 6
    30 × 49 = 1470 → 1 4$_2$ 7 0

③ 196 + 1470 = 1666 → 1 6$_1$ 6 6

Grid Method

1. **Split** each number into units, tens, etc.
2. **Draw a grid.** Write the parts of one number along the top and the parts of the other number down the side.
3. **Multiply round the edge** to fill squares.
4. **Add up** numbers in squares.

EXAMPLE

Calculate 53 × 27.

① 53 = 50 + 3 and 27 = 20 + 7

②
×	50	3
20	1000	60
7	350	21

③ 50 × 20 = 1000
    3 × 20 = 60
    50 × 7 = 350
    3 × 7 = 21

④ 1000 + 60 + 350 + 21 = **1431**

Lattice Method

1. **Split** each number into digits.
2. **Draw a grid.** Write the digits of one number along the top and the digits of the other number down the side.
3. **Multiply round the edge** to fill squares, separating tens and units with **diagonal lines**.
4. **Add up** along diagonals to get the answer.

EXAMPLE

What is 65 × 32?

① 65 has 6 tens and 5 units
32 has 3 tens and 2 units

②③
     6   5
   1/1/
   /8/5 3
   1/1/
   /2/0 2

6 × 3 = 18
5 × 3 = 15
6 × 2 = 12
5 × 2 = 10

④ 1 10 8 0
   2$_1$ 0 8 0
So 65 × 32 = **2080**

This method is also known as Chinese or Gelosia multiplication.

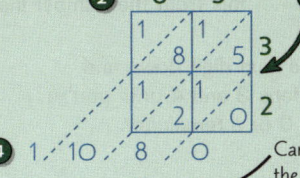

Carry the tens to the next column when the sum of a diagonal is two digits.

Section 1 — Numbers

Dividing without a Calculator

Four Steps for Short Division

1. Put the number you're dividing inside and the number you're dividing by outside.

2. List the first few multiples of the number you're dividing by.

3. Divide each digit below the line:
   - Write the result above the line.
   - Carry any remainder to the next digit.

4. Continue until there are no more numbers to divide into — the top line gives the final answer.

EXAMPLE

What is 375 ÷ 15?

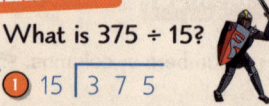

1. 15) 3 7 5

2. Multiples of 15:
   1 × 15 = 15   4 × 15 = 60
   2 × 15 = 30   5 × 15 = 75
   3 × 15 = 45   6 × 15 = 90

3. 0
   15) 3 7 5   15 won't go into 3

    0 2
   15) 3 7⁷5   37 ÷ 15 = 2 remainder 7

4. 0 2 5
   15) 3 7⁷5   75 ÷ 15 = 5

   So 375 ÷ 15 = 25

Six Steps for Long Division

1. Put the number you're dividing inside and the number you're dividing by outside.

2. List the first few multiples of the number you're dividing by.

3. Divide the digits below the line and write the result above the line.

4. Multiply the result by the number outside and subtract this from the number inside.

5. Move the next digit down and repeat steps 3 and 4 until you're left with 0 or a remainder.

6. Write out the result with the remainder (if there is one).

EXAMPLE

Work out 724 ÷ 21.

1. 21) 7 2 4

2. Multiples of 21:
   1 × 21 = 21   3 × 21 = 63
   2 × 21 = 42   4 × 21 = 84

3. 7 doesn't divide by 21, but 21 goes into 72 three times

    0 3 4
   21) 7 2 4
4. 3 × 21 = 63 → − 6 3
                    9 4
   4 × 21 = 84 → − 8 4
                    1 0   5.

   10 doesn't divide by 21, so it's a remainder

6. So 724 ÷ 21 = 34 remainder 10

Section 1 — Numbers

Special Types of Number

Negative Numbers on a Number Line

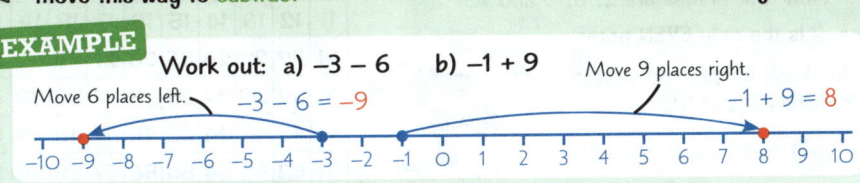

⟵ numbers get lower this way   numbers get higher this way ⟹
–10 –9 –8 –7 –6 –5 –4 –3 –2 –1 0 1 2 3 4 5 6 7 8 9 10
⟵ move this way to subtract   move this way to add ⟹

EXAMPLE

Work out: a) –3 – 6   b) –1 + 9

Move 6 places left. $-3 - 6 = -9$ Move 9 places right. $-1 + 9 = 8$

Four Rules for Combining Signs

① + + makes +   ③ + – makes –
② – + makes –   ④ – – makes +

Use when:
- Multiplying or dividing
- Two signs are next to each other

EXAMPLE

Calculate: (invisible + sign)

a) -6×9 – + makes – $-6 \times 9 = -54$
b) $-8 \div -4$ – – makes + $-8 \div -4 = 2$
c) $11 + -7$ + – makes – $11 - 7 = 4$
d) $-8 - -5$ – – makes + $-8 + 5 = -3$

Calculations with Even and Odd Numbers

5 + 7 = 12 ?

EVEN NUMBER — divides by 2. Ends in 0, 2, 4, 6 or 8.
ODD NUMBER — doesn't divide by 2. Ends in 1, 3, 5, 7 or 9.

① **ADDING**
odd + odd = even
even + even = even
odd + even = odd
even + odd = odd

② **SUBTRACTING**
odd – odd = even
even – even = even
odd – even = odd
even – odd = odd

③ **MULTIPLYING**
odd × odd = odd
even × even = even
odd × even = even
even × odd = even

Square Numbers

SQUARE NUMBER — result of multiplying whole number by itself.

$1^2 = 1 \times 1 = 1$ $4^2 = 4 \times 4 = 16$
$2^2 = 2 \times 2 = 4$ $5^2 = 5 \times 5 = 25$
$3^2 = 3 \times 3 = 9$ $6^2 = 6 \times 6 = 36$

Cube Numbers

CUBE NUMBER — result of multiplying whole number by itself, then by itself again.

$1^3 = 1 \times 1 \times 1 = 1$ $4^3 = 4 \times 4 \times 4 = 64$
$2^3 = 2 \times 2 \times 2 = 8$ $5^3 = 5 \times 5 \times 5 = 125$
$3^3 = 3 \times 3 \times 3 = 27$ $6^3 = 6 \times 6 \times 6 = 216$

Section 1 — Numbers

Prime Numbers, Multiples and Factors

Finding Prime Numbers

PRIME NUMBER — can be divided exactly by only itself and 1.
- 1 is NOT prime.
- First four primes are 2, 3, 5 and 7.
- 2 is the only EVEN prime.

To check for prime numbers between 8 and 100:

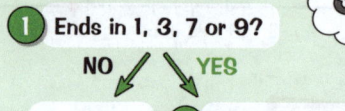

1. Ends in 1, 3, 7 or 9?
   - NO → not prime
   - YES → 2. Divides by 3 or 7?
     - NO → PRIME
     - YES → not prime

This step works for checking primes between 8 and 120.

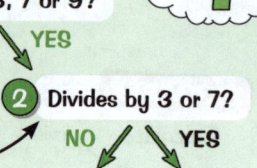

1	2	3	4	5	6	7	8	9	10
11	12	13	14	15	16	17	18	19	20
21	22	23	24	25	26	27	28	29	30
31	32	33	34	35	36	37	38	39	40
41	42	43	44	45	46	47	48	49	50
51	52	53	54	55	56	57	58	59	60
61	62	63	64	65	66	67	68	69	70
71	72	73	74	75	76	77	78	79	80
81	82	83	84	85	86	87	88	89	90
91	92	93	94	95	96	97	98	99	100

Finding Multiples

MULTIPLE — value in a number's times table (and beyond).

The first multiples of any number are just the first numbers in its times table.

EXAMPLE

a) Find the first six multiples of 10.
10, 20, 30, 40, 50, 60

b) Find the first eight multiples of 9.
9, 18, 27, 36, 45, 54, 63, 72

Four Steps to Find Factors

FACTOR — number that divides exactly into a given number.

1. List factors in pairs, starting with 1 × the number, then 2 ×, etc.
2. Cross out pairs that don't divide exactly.
3. Stop when a number is repeated.
4. Write factors out clearly.

EXAMPLE

Find all the factors of 42.

1.
   1 × 42
   2 × 21
   3 × 14
2.
   ~~4 ×~~
   ~~5 ×~~
   6 × 7
3. ~~7 × 6~~

Square numbers have repeated factors — e.g. 6 × 6 = 36

Stop here as 7 already appears in the list.

4. So the factors of 42 are:
1, 2, 3, 6, 7, 14, 21, 42

Section 1 — Numbers

Prime Factors, LCM and HCF

Four Steps to Find Prime Factors

PRIME FACTORISATION — writing a number as its prime factors multiplied together.

1. Put the number at the top and split into factors.
2. Circle each prime.
3. Keep going until only primes are left.
4. Write primes in order.

Repeated factors can be written as powers.

EXAMPLE

Find the prime factorisation of 360.

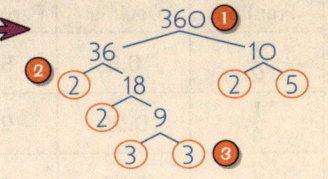

$$360 = 2 \times 2 \times 2 \times 3 \times 3 \times 5$$
$$= 2^3 \times 3^2 \times 5$$

Lovely crunchy meal

Lowest Common Multiple (LCM)

LCM — the smallest number that divides exactly by all numbers in question.

Find it in two steps:

1. List multiples of each number.
2. Find the smallest number that is in every list.

EXAMPLE

Find the LCM of 9 and 12.

1. Multiples of 9 are:
   9, 18, 27, 36, 45, 54...

   Multiples of 12 are:
   12, 24, 36, 48...

2. Smallest in both is 36, so LCM = 36

Highest Common Factor (HCF)

HCF — the biggest number that divides exactly into all numbers in question.

Find it in two steps:

1. List factors of each number.
2. Find the biggest number that is in every list.

EXAMPLE

Find the HCF of 12, 42 and 66.

1. Factors of 12 are:
   1, 2, 3, 4, 6, 12

   Factors of 42 are:
   1, 2, 3, 6, 7, 14, 21, 42

   Factors of 66 are:
   1, 2, 3, 6, 11, 22, 33, 66

2. Biggest factor in each list is 6, so HCF = 6

Section 1 — Numbers

Fractions, Decimals and Percentages

Common Conversions

Fraction	Decimal	Percentage
$\frac{1}{2}$	0.5	50%
$\frac{1}{4}$	0.25	25%
$\frac{3}{4}$	0.75	75%
$\frac{1}{3}$	0.333...	$33\frac{1}{3}$%
$\frac{2}{3}$	0.666...	$66\frac{2}{3}$%

Fraction	Decimal	Percentage
$\frac{1}{10}$	0.1	10%
$\frac{2}{10}$	0.2	20%
$\frac{1}{5}$	0.2	20%
$\frac{2}{5}$	0.4	40%

0.333... and 0.666... are recurring decimals. They carry on repeating forever and can be written as $0.\dot{3}$ and $0.\dot{6}$.

How to Convert

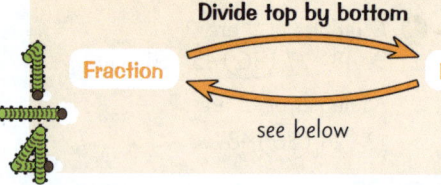

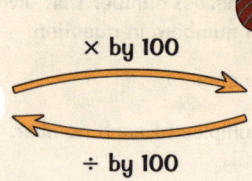

Fraction → Divide top by bottom → Decimal → × by 100 → Percentage

Decimal → see below → Fraction

Percentage → ÷ by 100 → Decimal

Converting Decimals to Fractions

1. Put digits **after decimal point** on the top.
2. Put a **power of 10** on the bottom with the same number of zeros as there were decimal places.
3. Simplify if you can (see next page).

EXAMPLE

Convert these decimals to fractions:
a) 0.5   b) 0.94   c) 0.325

a) 0.5 → ① ② $\frac{5}{10}$ → ③ $\frac{1}{2}$
1 digit on top so 10 on the bottom.

b) 0.94 → ① ② $\frac{94}{100}$ → ③ $\frac{47}{50}$
2 digits on top so 100 on the bottom.

c) 0.325 → ① ② $\frac{325}{1000}$ → ③ $\frac{13}{40}$
3 digits on top so 1000 on the bottom.

Section 1 — Numbers

Fractions

Equivalent Fractions

EQUIVALENT FRACTION — same value, different numbers on top and bottom.

To simplify a fraction, divide top and bottom by the same number until they won't divide any more.

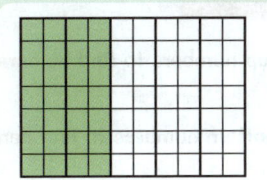

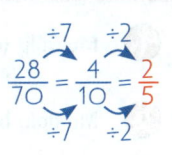

$$\frac{28}{70} \xrightarrow{\div 7} = \frac{4}{10} \xrightarrow{\div 2} = \frac{2}{5}$$

Ordering Fractions

1. Find a number that both bottom numbers go into.
2. Write each fraction as an equivalent fraction with the same bottom number.
3. See which fraction has the larger top number.

EXAMPLE

Which is bigger, $\frac{4}{5}$ or $\frac{5}{7}$?

1. 5 and 7 both go into 35.
2. $\frac{4}{5} \xrightarrow{\times 7} = \frac{28}{35}$ $\frac{5}{7} \xrightarrow{\times 5} = \frac{25}{35}$
3. $\frac{28}{35}$ is bigger than $\frac{25}{35}$

So $\frac{4}{5}$ is bigger.

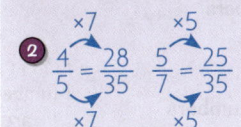

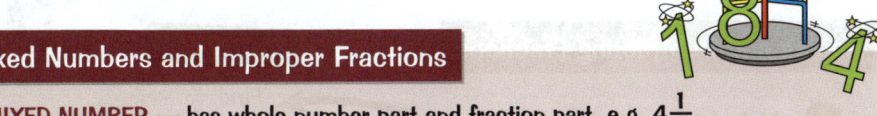

Mixed Numbers and Improper Fractions

MIXED NUMBER — has whole number part and fraction part, e.g. $4\frac{1}{8}$.

IMPROPER FRACTION — top number is larger than bottom number, e.g. $\frac{13}{4}$.

To write mixed numbers as improper fractions:

1. Write as an addition.
2. Turn whole number part into a fraction.
3. Add together.

EXAMPLE

What is $3\frac{2}{3}$ as an improper fraction?

$$3\frac{2}{3} = 3 + \frac{2}{3} = \frac{9}{3} + \frac{2}{3} = \frac{11}{3}$$

To write improper fractions as mixed numbers:

1. Divide top by bottom.
2. Answer is whole number part, remainder goes on top of fraction part.

EXAMPLE

Write $\frac{27}{4}$ as a mixed number.

1. $27 \div 4 = 6$ remainder 3
2. So $\frac{27}{4} = 6\frac{3}{4}$

Section 1 — Numbers

Fraction Calculations

Multiplying Fractions

1. Multiply top numbers to find numerator.
2. Multiply bottom numbers to find denominator.

$$\frac{4}{9} \times \frac{2}{3} = \frac{4 \times 2}{9 \times 3} = \frac{8}{27}$$

Dividing Fractions

1. Turn 2nd fraction upside down, then change ÷ to ×.
2. Multiply top numbers to find numerator.
3. Multiply bottom numbers to find denominator.

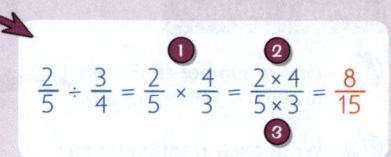

$$\frac{2}{5} \div \frac{3}{4} = \frac{2}{5} \times \frac{4}{3} = \frac{2 \times 4}{5 \times 3} = \frac{8}{15}$$

Numbers turned upside down are called reciprocals.

Adding and Subtracting Fractions

1. Make bottom numbers the same.
2. Add/subtract the top numbers only.

EXAMPLE

Find $\frac{6}{7} - \frac{2}{3}$.

① $\frac{6}{7} - \frac{2}{3} = \frac{18}{21} - \frac{14}{21}$

② $= \frac{18 - 14}{21} = \frac{4}{21}$

Finding Fractions of Amounts

1. Multiply by the top number.
2. Divide by the bottom number.

$\frac{4}{5}$ of 80 = (80 × 4) ÷ 5
= 320 ÷ 5 = 64

Divide then multiply if it's easier.

Expressing as a Fraction

1. Write 1st number over 2nd.
2. Cancel down.

72 as a fraction of 96

$$\frac{72}{96} \xrightarrow{\div 8} \frac{9}{12} \xrightarrow{\div 3} \frac{3}{4}$$

If the 1st number is bigger, the answer will be greater than 1.

Section 1 — Numbers

Percentages

Finding Percentages with a Calculator

'Per cent' means 'out of 100'.   E.g. 40% means '40 out of 100' = $\frac{40}{100}$ = 0.4

Two steps for '% of' questions using a calculator:

1. Change percentage to a **decimal**.
2. Replace 'of' with × and multiply.

EXAMPLE

Find 24% of 60.
1. 24% = 24 ÷ 100 = 0.24
2. 0.24 × 60 = 14.4

Finding Percentages without a Calculator

1. **Split up** into smaller percentages.
2. Find the values of the smaller percentages.
3. **Combine** to get the percentage asked for.

EXAMPLE

Find 45% of 80 without using a calculator.
1. 45% = (4 × 10%) + 5%
2. 10% of 80 = 80 ÷ 10 = 8
   5% of 80 = 8 ÷ 2 = 4
   5% is half of 10%.
3. 45% of 80 = (4 × 8) + 4 = 36

One Number as a Percentage of Another

1. Divide the first number by the second number.
2. Multiply by 100.

Kian gave 110%, but only 5% of the time.

EXAMPLE

Write 18 as a percentage of 72.
1. 18 ÷ 72 = 0.25
2. 0.25 × 100 = 25%

EXAMPLE

Write 25 as a percentage of 20.
1. 25 ÷ 20 = 1.25
2. 1.25 × 100 = 125%

A decimal greater than 1 gives a percentage greater than 100%.

Section 1 — Numbers

Rounding Numbers

Two Steps to Round to Decimal Places

1. Identify the position of the **last digit** from the number of decimal places.

2. Look at the digit to the right — the **decider**.
   - If the decider is **5 or more**, round **up** the last digit.
   - If the decider is **4 or less**, leave the last digit **as it is**.

To round up a 9, replace it with 0 and add 1 to the digit on the left.

EXAMPLE

Round 17.2416 to 1 decimal place.

1. 17.②416 — Circle the last digit.
2. The decider is 4, so the last digit stays as it is.
   17.2416 = 17.2 to 1 d.p.

EXAMPLE

Round 8.2962 to 2 decimal places.

1. 8.2⑨62 — Circle the last digit.
2. The decider is 6, so the last digit gets rounded up.
   8.2962 = 8.30 to 2 d.p.

It's to 2 d.p., so put 8.30 not 8.3.

Three Steps to Round to Significant Figures

The **1st significant figure (s.f.)** is the first digit that **isn't zero**. Each digit after it (including zeros) is another significant figure.

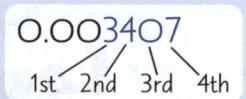

0.003407
1st 2nd 3rd 4th

1. Identify the position of the **last digit** in the rounded number.

2. Look at the digit to the right — the **decider**.
   - If the decider is **5 or more**, round **up** the last digit.
   - If the decider is **4 or less**, leave the last digit **as it is**.

3. Fill spaces **before** the decimal point with **zeros**.

EXAMPLE

Round 6835 to 2 significant figures.

1. 6⑧35 — Circle the last digit.
2. The decider is 3, so the last digit stays as it is.
3. 6835 = 6800 to 2 s.f.

Fill 2 spaces with zeros.

EXAMPLE

Round 0.07026 to 3 s.f.

1. 0.070②6 — Circle the last digit.
2. The decider is 6, so the last digit rounds up to 3.
3. 0.07026 = 0.0703 to 3 s.f.

Section 1 — Numbers

Rounding and Estimation

Rounding to the Nearest...

... whole number, ten, hundred, etc.

1. Identify the position of the **last digit** in the rounded number.
   This could be units place, tens place, etc.

2. Look at the digit to the right — the **decider**.
   - If the decider is **5 or more**, round **up** the last digit.
   - If the decider is **4 or less**, leave the last digit **as it is**.

3. Fill spaces **before** the decimal point with **zeros**.

EXAMPLE

Round 382 to the nearest hundred.

1. ③82 — Circle the last digit.
2. The decider is 8, so the last digit rounds up to 4.
3. 382 = 400 to nearest 100
   — Fill 2 spaces with zeros.

EXAMPLE

Round 2.385 to the nearest whole number.

1. ②.385 — Circle the last digit.
2. The decider is 3, so the last digit stays as it is.
3. 2.385 = 2 to nearest whole number

Two Steps to Calculate Error

ERROR — difference between rounded value and actual value.

1. Round the number to given accuracy.
2. Subtract actual value from rounded value.

EXAMPLE

What is the error when 3.15 is given to 1 decimal place?

1. 3.15 = 3.2 to 1 d.p.
2. 3.2 − 3.15 = 0.05

Estimating Calculations

ESTIMATING — working out an approximate answer.

1. Round to convenient numbers — usually 1 s.f.
2. Work out answer using rounded numbers.

EXAMPLE

Estimate the value of $\frac{19.25 \times 2.2}{5.23}$.

$$\frac{19.25 \times 2.2}{5.23} \approx \frac{20 \times 2}{5}$$

$$= \frac{40}{5} = 8$$

≈ means 'is approximately equal to'.

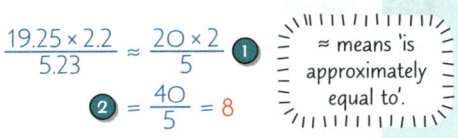

Section 1 — Numbers

Powers and Roots

Four Rules for Powers

POWERS — numbers multiplied by themselves. ➡ $2^5 = 2 \times 2 \times 2 \times 2 \times 2$

1. **Powers of ten** — the power tells you how many **zeros**. $10^4 = 10\,000$
2. Anything to the **power 1** is itself. $5^1 = 5$
3. Anything to the **power 0** is 1. $7^0 = 1$
4. **1** to any power is **1**. $1^{99} = 1$

Use a button on your calculator to work out powers — it may look like $x^{\blacksquare}$ or y^x.

Multiplying and Dividing with Powers

Letters obey the same rules as numbers.

These rules are only true for powers of the **same number**:

Multiplying — **ADD** the powers.
$6^3 \times 6^{10} = 6^{3+10} = 6^{13}$
$x^2 \times x^3 = x^{3+2} = x^5$

Dividing — **SUBTRACT** the powers.
$8^9 \div 8^7 = 8^{9-7} = 8^2$
$y^8 \div y^4 = y^{8-4} = y^4$

Square Roots

SQUARED — multiplied by itself.

SQUARE ROOT ($\sqrt{}$) — the reverse process, e.g. $3^2 = 9$, so $\sqrt{9} = 3$.

Think of 'square root' as:

'What number times by itself gives...'

All numbers also have a **negative** square root. It's the '−' version of the positive one.

EXAMPLE

Find both square roots of 49.

$49 = 7 \times 7$, so positive square root $= 7$ and negative square root $= -7$.

Cube Roots

CUBED — multiplied by itself and then by itself again.

CUBE ROOT ($\sqrt[3]{}$) — the reverse process, e.g. $4^3 = 64$, so $\sqrt[3]{64} = 4$.

Think of 'cube root' as:

'What number times by itself and then by itself again gives...'

EXAMPLE

What is $\sqrt[3]{8}$?

$8 = 2 \times 2 \times 2$, so $\sqrt[3]{8} = 2$.

Higher roots are found in the same way — e.g. $\sqrt[7]{}$ is the reverse process of 'to the power 7'.

Section 2 — Algebra and Graphs

Algebra Basics

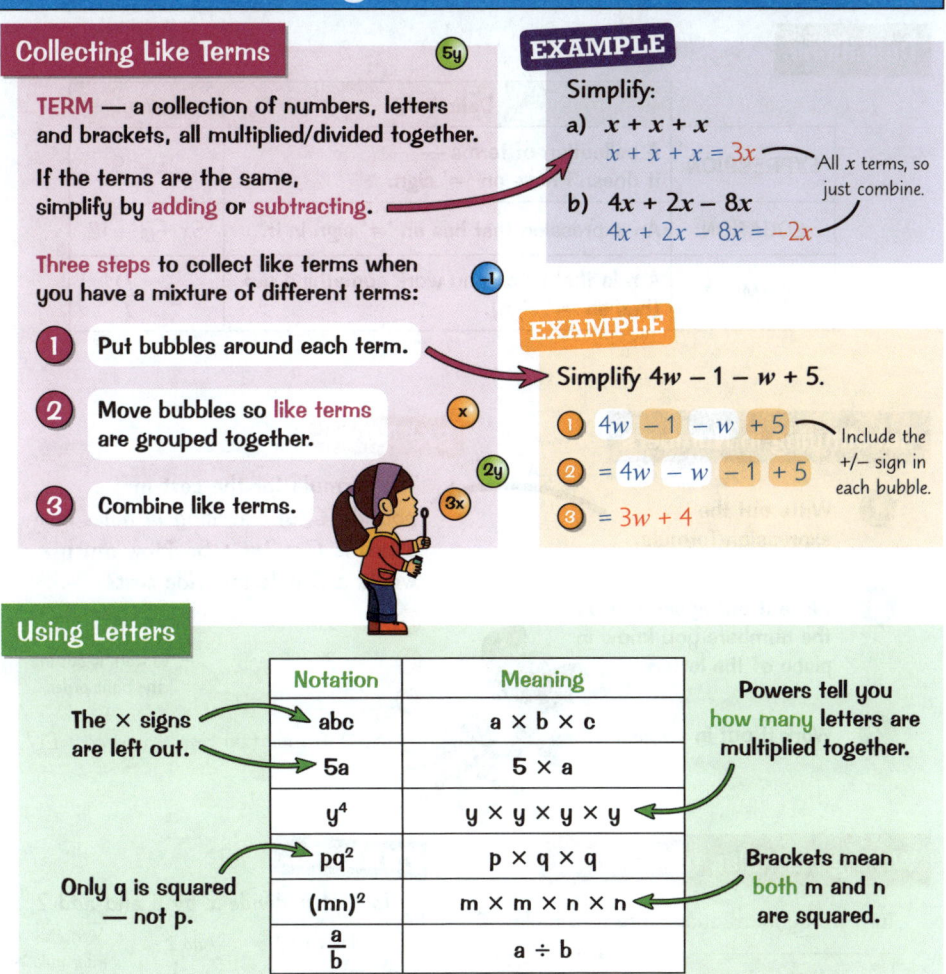

Collecting Like Terms

TERM — a collection of numbers, letters and brackets, all multiplied/divided together.

If the terms are the same, simplify by adding or subtracting.

Three steps to collect like terms when you have a mixture of different terms:

1. Put bubbles around each term.
2. Move bubbles so like terms are grouped together.
3. Combine like terms.

EXAMPLE

Simplify:
a) $x + x + x$
$x + x + x = 3x$ — All x terms, so just combine.

b) $4x + 2x - 8x$
$4x + 2x - 8x = -2x$

EXAMPLE

Simplify $4w - 1 - w + 5$.

1. $4w$ -1 $-w$ $+5$ — Include the +/− sign in each bubble.
2. $= 4w$ $-w$ -1 $+5$
3. $= 3w + 4$

Using Letters

Notation	Meaning
abc	a × b × c
5a	5 × a
y^4	y × y × y × y
pq^2	p × q × q
$(mn)^2$	m × m × n × n
$\frac{a}{b}$	a ÷ b

The × signs are left out.

Powers tell you how many letters are multiplied together.

Only q is squared — not p.

Brackets mean both m and n are squared.

Multiplying Single Brackets

Multiply each term inside the bracket by the bit outside the bracket.

$4(x - 3) = (4 \times x) + (4 \times -3)$
$= 4x - 12$

If you have a letter multiplied by itself, write it as a power.

$a(3a + 8) = (a \times 3a) + (a \times 8)$
$= 3a^2 + 8a$

Formulas

Definitions

	Definition	Example
EXPRESSION	A collection of terms — it doesn't have an '=' sign.	$2x - 9$
EQUATION	An expression that has an '=' sign in it.	$5x + 3 = 18$
FORMULA	A rule that helps you work something out (has an '=' sign).	$S = \dfrac{D}{T}$

Substituting in Numbers

1. Write out the expression/formula.
2. Write it out again, but put the numbers you know in place of the letters.
3. Work it out in stages.

EXAMPLE

The formula for the cost in pounds, C, of travelling m miles in a taxi is $C = 2m + 5$. How much would a 6-mile taxi ride cost?

1. $C = 2m + 5$
2. $C = 2 \times 6 + 5$ — Use BODMAS to work it out in the right order.
3. $C = 12 + 5 = 17$

So a 6-mile taxi ride would cost £17.

Writing Formulas from Words

Turn **wordy instructions** into a formula:

Instruction	Example
Add/subtract a number	$x + 5$ or $x - 1$
Multiply x	$4x$
Divide x	$\dfrac{x}{2}$
Square/square root x	x^2 or $\sqrt{x}$
Cube x	x^3

Use **letters** to label things when the formula is given in words.

EXAMPLE

To find y, divide x by 3 and add 2.

Divide x by 3. Add 2. Write as a formula.

$x \rightarrow \dfrac{x}{3} \rightarrow \dfrac{x}{3} + 2 \rightarrow y = \dfrac{x}{3} + 2$

EXAMPLE

To find the number of points (p) you score in a game, square the number of counters (c), then subtract 4. Write a formula for the points scored.

Square c. Subtract 4. Write as a formula.

$c \rightarrow c^2 \rightarrow c^2 - 4 \rightarrow p = c^2 - 4$

Solving Equations

Three Rules for Solving Equations

1. Do the same thing to both sides of the equation.
2. Do the opposite operation to get rid of things you don't want.
   - \+ is the opposite of −
   - × is the opposite of ÷
3. Keep going until you have a letter on its own.

EXAMPLE

Solve $x + 7 = 2$ — The opposite of '+7' is '−7'.
① $x + 7 - 7 = 2 - 7$
③ $x = -5$

EXAMPLE

Solve $4x = 32$ — $4x$ means $4 \times x$ — so do the opposite, which is '÷4'.
① $4x \div 4 = 32 \div 4$
③ $x = 8$

Two-Step Equations

If there's an x term and a number on the same side of the equation:

1. Add/subtract the number.
2. Multiply or divide to get '$x = ...$'.

EXAMPLE

Solve $6x + 2 = 26$ — Subtract 2 from both sides.
① $6x + 2 - 2 = 26 - 2$
   $6x = 24$
② $6x \div 6 = 24 \div 6$ — Divide both sides by 6.
   $x = 4$

EXAMPLE

Solve $\frac{x}{3} - 4 = 1$ — Add 4 to both sides.
① $\frac{x}{3} - 4 + 4 = 1 + 4$
   $\frac{x}{3} = 5$
② $\frac{x}{3} \times 3 = 5 \times 3$ — Multiply both sides by 3.
   $x = 15$

When x is on Both Sides

1. Get all the x's on one side of =, and all the numbers on the other.
2. Multiply or divide to get '$x = ...$'.

EXAMPLE

Solve $4x - 9 = 5 - 3x$ — Add 9 to both sides.
① $4x - 9 + 9 = 5 - 3x + 9$
   $4x = 14 - 3x$
   $4x + 3x = 14 - 3x + 3x$ — Add 3x to both sides.
   $7x = 14$
② $7x \div 7 = 14 \div 7$ — Divide both sides by 7.
   $x = 2$

Section 2 — Algebra and Graphs

Number Patterns and Sequences

Number Patterns

To find the rule for number patterns, work out how to get from one term to the next.

Geometric sequins

ARITHMETIC SEQUENCES — adding or subtracting the same number:

+6 +6 +6
7 13 19 25 ...
Rule: Add 6 to the previous term

−3 −3 −3
20 17 14 11 ...
Rule: Subtract 3 from the previous term

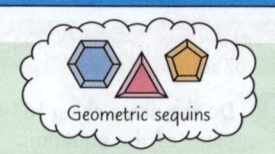

GEOMETRIC SEQUENCES — multiplying or dividing by the same number:

×4 ×4 ×4
1 4 16 64 ...
Rule: Multiply previous term by 4

÷2 ÷2 ÷2
96 48 24 12 ...
Rule: Divide previous term by 2

Shape Patterns

Work out what to do to continue the pattern.

EXAMPLE

Draw the next pattern in the sequence on the right.

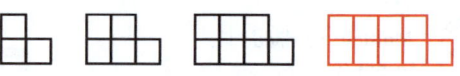

Rule: Add two squares each time.

nth Term of an Arithmetic Sequence

nth TERM — a rule that gives the terms in a sequence when you put in different 'n' values.

1. Find the number you add/subtract each time — the common difference.
2. Multiply the common difference by n and list the values.
3. Work out what to add or subtract to get to the term.
4. Put both bits together.
5. Check the formula by putting first few values of n back in.

If the sequence is decreasing, the common difference will be negative.

EXAMPLE

Find the nth term of the sequence 5, 8, 11, 14 ...

1. $8 − 5 = 3$, $11 − 8 = 3$, ...
   Common difference = 3

2. $3n$: 3   6   9   12
3.   +2 +2 +2 +2
   Term: 5   8   11 14

4. So nth term is $3n + 2$

5. $n = 1$: $3 × 1 + 2 = 5$ ✓
   $n = 2$: $3 × 2 + 2 = 8$ ✓

Section 2 — Algebra and Graphs

Coordinates and Straight-Line Graphs

Coordinate Grid and Quadrants

x-AXIS — goes from left to right. The horizontal axis.

y-AXIS — goes from bottom to top. The vertical axis.

ORIGIN — point with coordinates (0, 0) where the x- and y-axes cross.

The x- and y-coordinates can be positive or negative, depending on which of the four **quadrants** (regions) you're in:

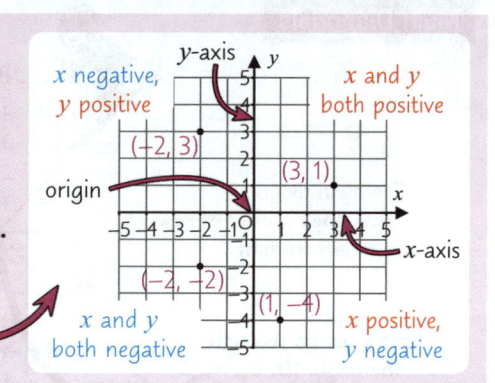

- x negative, y positive
- x and y both positive
- x and y both negative
- x positive, y negative

Reading Coordinates

Coordinates are written as:

$$(x, y)$$

They're in alphabetical order.

1. Read off x-axis to find x-coordinate.
2. Read off y-axis to find y-coordinate.

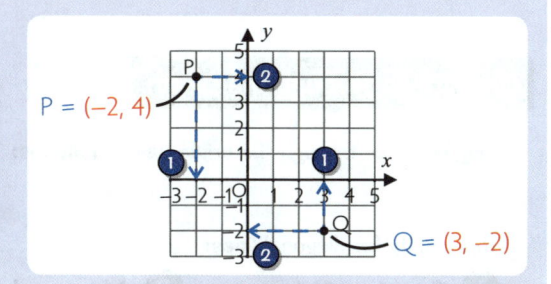

P = (−2, 4)

Q = (3, −2)

Vertical Lines

$$x = a$$

'a' is just a number.

Vertical lines go through 'a' on x-axis.

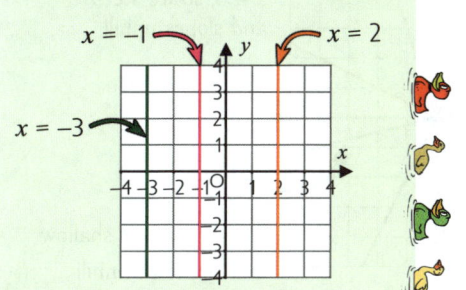

$x = -1$, $x = 2$, $x = -3$

The y-axis is the line $x = 0$.

Horizontal Lines

$$y = a$$

Horizontal lines go through 'a' on y-axis.

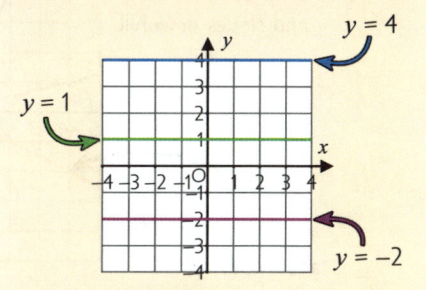

$y = 4$, $y = 1$, $y = -2$

The x-axis is the line $y = 0$.

Section 2 — Algebra and Graphs

Straight-Line Graphs

Main Diagonals

y = x

The main diagonal that goes uphill from left to right.

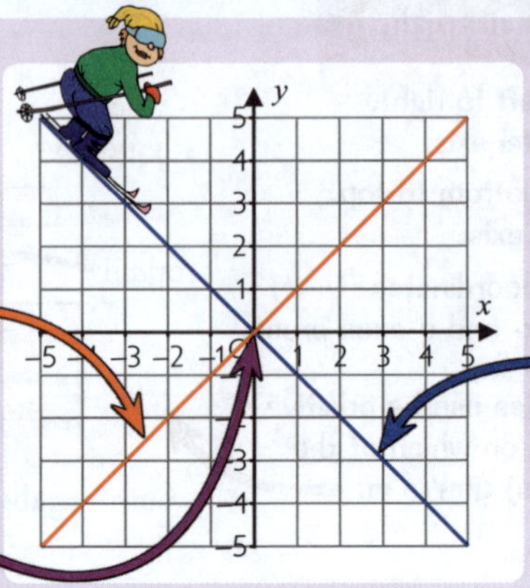

Both lines go through the origin (0, 0).

y = −x

The main diagonal that goes downhill from left to right.

Other Lines Through the Origin

Diagonal lines through the origin have equations: **y = ax** or **y = −ax**

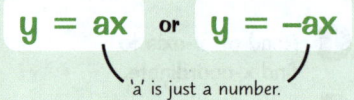

'a' is just a number.

Three facts for diagonal lines:

1. The value of 'a' (the gradient) tells you the steepness.

2. A bigger value of 'a' means a steeper line.

3. A negative gradient (i.e. a minus sign) means the line slopes downhill from left to right.

$y = -2x$:
a = −2, so it's steep and slopes downhill.

$y = 3x$:
a = 3, so it's steep and slopes uphill.

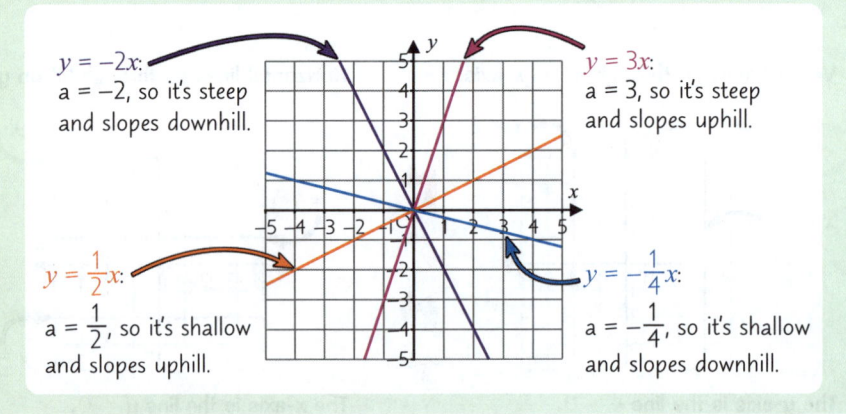

$y = \frac{1}{2}x$:
a = $\frac{1}{2}$, so it's shallow and slopes uphill.

$y = -\frac{1}{4}x$:
a = $-\frac{1}{4}$, so it's shallow and slopes downhill.

Section 2 — Algebra and Graphs

Straight-Line Graphs and Plotting

All Other Straight Lines

Straight lines only have x-terms, y-terms and number terms.

If there are any other terms, such as x^2, xy or $\frac{1}{x}$, it's not a straight line.

Straight lines don't need all of these — e.g. $y = x$ is a straight line but has no number term.

Straight lines:

$2x = y + 4$
$y = 3x - 2$
$x + 5y + 7 = 0$
$4x = 3$

All only contain x, y and number terms, so they're all straight lines ✓

NOT straight lines:

$xy = 2$ — has an xy term ✗
$x^2 - y^2 = 1$ — has an x^2 and y^2 term ✗
$x - \frac{2}{y} = 5$ — has a $\frac{2}{y}$ term ✗
$y = 4 - x^3$ — has an x^3 term ✗

Four Steps for Plotting Straight Lines

① Choose three x-values and put in a table.

Pick easy values — avoid negatives if you can.

② Put the x-values into the equation and work out the y-values.

③ Plot each pair of x- and y-values on the grid.

④ Draw a straight line through the points.

Extend the line if you need to.

EXAMPLE

Draw the graph $y = 2x - 4$ for values of x from 0 to 6.

① ②

x	0	3	6
y	−4	2	8

E.g. when $x = 3$,
$y = 2(3) - 4$
$= 6 - 4 = 2$

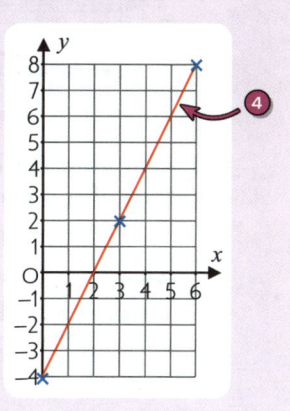

First, straight lines. Then the end of the world...

Section 2 — Algebra and Graphs

Reading Off Graphs

Three Steps for Reading Off Graphs

1. Draw a line from the value you want on one axis.
2. When you reach the **line**, go to the other axis.
3. Read off the value from this axis.

EXAMPLE

Use the graph below to find the value of y when $x = 6$.

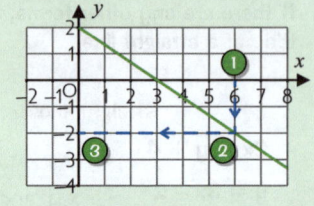

Go down from $x = 6$: $y = -2$

Curved Graphs

Use the same method for curved graphs. If the answer isn't a whole number, you'll need to **estimate**.

EXAMPLE

The graph below shows the population of rabbits in a forest over time.

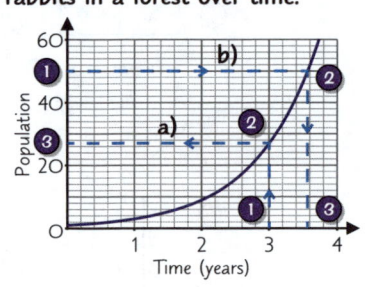

a) How many rabbits are there after 3 years?
Go up from 3 years: **27 rabbits**

b) After how many years are there 50 rabbits?
Go across from 50 rabbits: **Approximately 3.6 years**

EXAMPLE

Look at the graph below.

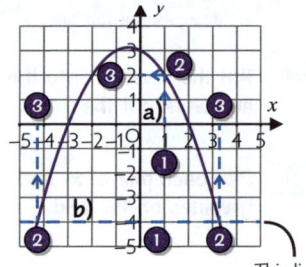

a) Find y when $x = 1$.
Go up from $x = 1$: **$y = 2$**

b) Find both values of x when $y = -4$.
Go across from $y = -4$: **$x \approx -4.3$ and $x \approx 3.3$**

This line crosses the graph twice.

Section 2 — Algebra and Graphs

Travel and Conversion Graphs

Travel Graphs

① Travel graphs have **distance** on the y-axis and **time** on the x-axis.

② Flat sections = **stopped**.

③ Steeper graph = faster **speed**.

④ Graph going up = **travelling away**.

⑤ Graph going down = **coming back**.

The travel graph below shows Amir's afternoon walk.

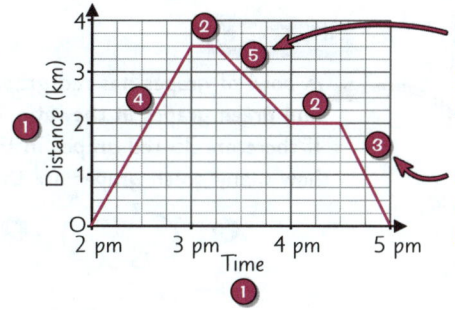

He comes back when the graph goes down, so Amir's return journey starts at **3:15 pm**.

Amir walks fastest when the graph is steepest, so he walks fastest between **4:30 pm and 5 pm**.

Conversion Graphs

Conker's conversion was only partially successful...

CONVERSION GRAPHS — show how to convert between units.

Read off conversion graphs using the same method as other graphs.

EXAMPLE

This graph can be used to convert between pounds (lb) and kilograms (kg).

a) What is 5 kg in pounds?
Go across from 5 kg: **5 kg = 11 lb**

b) To the nearest kg, estimate how many kg are in 18 lb.
Go up from 18 lb:
To the nearest kg, this is **8 kg**.

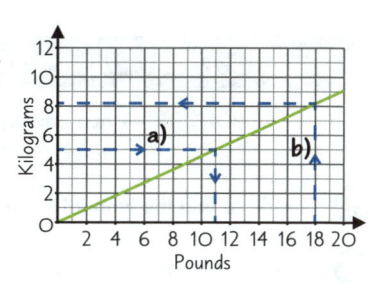

Section 2 — Algebra and Graphs

Ratios and Proportion

Two Steps to Simplify Ratios

1. **Divide** all numbers by the same thing.
2. **Keep going** until you can't divide any further.

After step 2, ratio is in **simplest form**.

EXAMPLE

Simplify these ratios: a) 6:12   b) 66:84

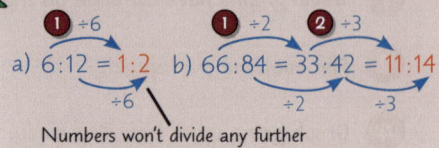

a) ①÷6: 6:12 = 1:2 (÷6)

b) ①÷2: 66:84 = 33:42 (÷2) ②÷3: = 11:14 (÷3)

Numbers won't divide any further so you don't need step 2.

Two Steps to Scale Up Ratios

1. Work out what one side of the ratio is **multiplied by** to get its **actual value**.
2. **Multiply** the other side by this number.

EXAMPLE

A bowl of grapes has red grapes and green grapes in the ratio 7:10. If there are 35 red grapes in the bowl, how many green grapes are there?

① ×5   7:10   ×5 ②
          35:50

So there are **50** green grapes

Three Steps for Proportional Division

1. **Add up** the parts.
2. **Divide** to find **one part**.
3. **Multiply** to find the **amounts**.

EXAMPLE

Sunita and Eric share a bunch of 50 flowers in the ratio 2:3. How many flowers does Eric get?

① 2 + 3 = 5 parts
② 1 part = 50 ÷ 5 = 10 flowers
③ 3 parts = 3 × 10 = 30 flowers

Two Steps for Direct Proportion Questions

DIRECT PROPORTION — two amounts increase or decrease together.

1. **Divide** to find the amount for **one thing**.
2. **Multiply** to find the amount for the number of things you want.

EXAMPLE

4 people can knit 12 hats per day. How many hats per day could 9 people knit?

① 1 person could knit
   12 ÷ 4 = 3 hats per day
② 9 people could knit
   3 × 9 = 27 hats per day

Proportion Problems

Two Steps for Scaling Recipes

1. **Divide** to find the amount for **one person**.
2. **Multiply** to find the amount for the number of people you want.

EXAMPLE

A chilli recipe for 4 people uses 240 g of kidney beans. How many grams of kidney beans are needed to make chilli for 10 people?

1. For 1 person you need
   240 g ÷ 4 = **60 g** of kidney beans
2. For 10 people you need
   60 g × 10 = **600 g** of kidney beans

Finding the Amount Per Penny

1. **Convert** prices in £ to pence.
2. For each item, **divide** amount by price in pence to get amount **per penny**.
3. **Compare** amounts per penny to find the best value.

More per penny means better value for money.

EXAMPLE

A 400 g tub of ice cream costs £2.50.
A 750 g tub of ice cream costs £3.75.
Which tub is better value for money?

1. £2.50 = 250p
   £3.75 = 375p
   Amounts should be in the same units too.
2. 400 g ÷ 250p = 1.6 g per penny
   750 g ÷ 375p = 2 g per penny
3. The **750 g tub** is better value as you get more ice cream per penny.

Bob's Best Buys Definitely Not Dodgy

Finding the Price Per Unit

1. **Convert** prices in £ to pence.
2. For each item, **divide** price in pence by amount to get price **per unit**.
3. **Compare** amounts per unit to find the best value.

Lower cost per unit means better value for money.

EXAMPLE

A 250 ml bottle of squash costs £1.50.
A 400 ml bottle of squash costs £2.20.
Which bottle is better value for money?

1. £1.50 = 150p
   £2.20 = 220p
2. 150p ÷ 250 ml = 0.6p per ml
   220p ÷ 400 ml = 0.55p per ml
3. The **400 ml bottle** is better value as squash is cheaper per ml.

Section 3 — Ratio, Proportion and Rates of Change

Percentage Increase and Decrease

Finding the Percentage Change

1. **Divide by 100** to write percentage as a decimal.
2. **Multiply** decimal by original value.
3. **Add to/subtract** from original value.

EXAMPLE

Decrease £80 by 30%.

1. 30% = 30 ÷ 100 = 0.3
2. 0.3 × £80 = £24
3. £80 − £24 = £56

Add for an increase, subtract for a decrease.

The Multiplier Method

MULTIPLIER — decimal you multiply original value by to increase/decrease it by a %.

% **increase** — multiplier is **greater** than 1
% **decrease** — multiplier is **less** than 1

Two steps for using multipliers:

1. Find **multiplier** — write % change as a decimal and add to/subtract from 1.
2. **Multiply** original value by multiplier.

EXAMPLE

Dan's rent is £650 a month. His rent increases by 5%. How much is his rent now?

1. 5% = 5 ÷ 100 = 0.05
   Multiplier for 5% increase
   = 1 + 0.05 = 1.05
2. New rent = £650 × 1.05
   = £682.50

Simple Interest

SIMPLE INTEREST — a % of the original value is paid at regular intervals (e.g. every year). The amount of interest doesn't change.

Three steps for simple interest questions:

1. Find the interest earned **each time**.
2. Multiply by the number of **intervals**.
3. **Add** to original value (if needed).

EXAMPLE

Cora puts £1500 in a savings account that pays 3% simple interest each year. How much will be in the account after 4 years?

1. 3% of £1500
   = 0.03 × £1500 = £45
2. 4 × £45 = £180 — Total interest earned
3. £1500 + £180 = £1680

Section 3 — Ratio, Proportion and Rates of Change

Units and Conversions

Metric Units

Length	Mass	Volume
1 cm = 10 mm	1 kg = 1000 g	1 litre = 1000 ml
1 m = 100 cm	1 tonne = 1000 kg	1 litre = 1000 cm^3
1 km = 1000 m		1 cm^3 = 1 ml

Bernard might have mixed up L and ml, but he was determined to make the best of it.

Three Steps for Converting Units

1. Write down conversion factor.
2. Multiply AND divide by it.
3. Choose sensible answer.

Think which unit there should be more of.

EXAMPLE

A llama is 170 cm tall. How tall is it in m?

1. 1 m = 100 cm, so conversion factor = 100
2. ~~170 × 100 = 17 000~~ — Cross out incorrect working.
   170 ÷ 100 = 1.7
3. 170 cm = 1.7 m — Add units.

Imperial Units

Length	Mass	Volume
e.g. inches, feet, yards, miles	e.g. ounces (oz), stones, pounds (lb), tons	e.g. pints, gallons

Metric-Imperial Conversions

For metric-imperial conversions, conversion factors will be given in the question.

EXAMPLE

A statue has a mass of 33 kg. Given that 1 kg ≈ 2.2 lb, find the mass of the statue in lb.

1. Conversion factor = 2.2 — From question
2. 33 × 2.2 = 72.6   ~~33 ÷ 2.2 = 15~~
3. 33 kg ≈ 72.6 lb — 1 kg is more than 1 lb, so there'll be more lb than kg

≈ means 'is approximately equal to'.

Section 3 — Ratio, Proportion and Rates of Change

Reading Timetables

12-Hour and 24-Hour Clocks

	12-hour clock	24-hour clock	
am means morning	12.00 am	00:00	← midnight
	6.30 am	06:30	
pm means afternoon or evening	12.00 pm	12:00	← noon
	6.30 pm	18:30	

Time Units

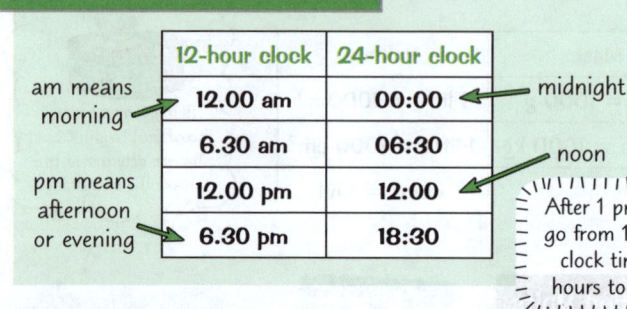

1 min = 60 secs	
1 hour = 60 mins	
1 day = 24 hours	

After 1 pm, add 12 hours to go from 12-hour to 24-hour clock times. Subtract 12 hours to go the other way.

Time Conversions

Convert the big units first, then **add** on any remaining small units.

Get rid of **decimals** by multiplying by the **conversion factor**.

When converting units, always check your answer is sensible.

EXAMPLE

Write: a) 255 mins in hours and mins
b) 2 mins 45 secs in seconds

a) 255 mins = 255 ÷ 60 = 4.25 hours
0.25 hours = 0.25 × 60 = 15 mins
255 mins = **4 hours 15 mins**

b) 2 mins = 2 × 60 = 120 seconds
120 + 45 = **165 seconds**

Time Calculations

1. **Split** time interval into **stages**.
2. **Convert** each stage to the **same units** (if needed).
3. **Add** to get total time.

EXAMPLE

A film starts at 19:45 and finishes at 22:10. How long is the film in minutes?

1. 19:45 → 20:00 → 22:00 → 22:10
   15 mins   2 hours   10 mins
2. 2 hours = 2 × 60 = 120 minutes
3. 15 + 120 + 10 = **145 minutes**

Reading Timetables

Here's part of a bus timetable. Read along rows and up/down columns to find answers.

First bus from Hill Top gets to Town Hall at **13:06** (or **1:06 pm**).

Hill Top	12 45	13 05	13 25
Beach Path	12 58	13 18	13 38
Town Hall	13 06	13 26	13 46

Hill Top to Town Hall takes **21 minutes**.

13:26 bus at Town Hall leaves Hill Top at **13:05** (or **1:05 pm**).

Section 3 — Ratio, Proportion and Rates of Change

Maps and Map Scales

Compass Directions

Compass points give directions.
There are **eight** main directions.

North (N), North-East (NE), East (E), South-East (SE), South (S), South-West (SW), West (W), North-West (NW)

There's 45° between each direction (and 90° between N, E, S and W).

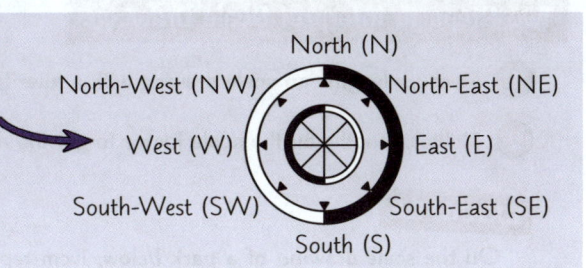

Three Types of Map Scale

① 1 cm = 5 km — means '1 cm on the map represents 5 km in real life'.

② |—| 0 km 2 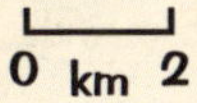 — the line is 1 cm long, so 1 cm on the map represents 2 km in real life.

③ 1 : 10 000 — means '1 cm on the map represents 10 000 cm in real life'.
10 000 cm = 100 m, so scale could be given as 1 cm = 100 m.

If the scale doesn't have units, use the same units for both sides then convert if needed.

Using Map Scales

To convert between maps and real life:

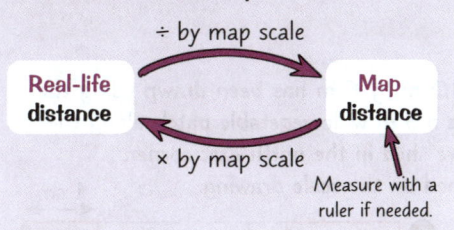

Real-life distance ⇄ Map distance
(÷ by map scale / × by map scale)

Measure with a ruler if needed.

Make sure scale is in the form '1 cm = ...'.

Check your answers look sensible — things shouldn't be too far apart on the map, or too close together in real life.

EXAMPLE

A map has a scale of 1 cm = 2.5 km.

a) Two towns are 8 cm apart on the map. How far apart are they in real life?

To go from a map distance to a real-life distance, multiply:

8 cm on the map represents
8 × 2.5 = **20** km in real life.

b) Two towns are 12.5 km apart in real life. How far apart will they be on the map?

To go from a real-life distance to a map distance, divide:

12.5 km in real life is represented by
12.5 ÷ 2.5 = **5** cm on the map.

Section 3 — Ratio, Proportion and Rates of Change

Scale Drawings

Two Steps to Interpret Scale Drawings

1. **Measure** lengths on scale drawing with a ruler (or use the grid if there is one).
2. **Multiply** lengths by the scale factor to get the real-life lengths.

EXAMPLE

On the scale drawing of a park below, 1 cm represents 5 m.
Find the real-life length and width of the lake and the terrace.

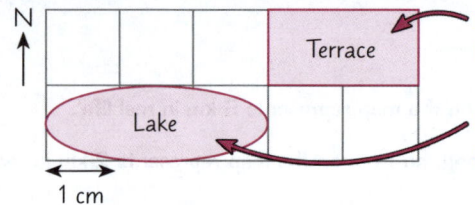

Diagram: 2 cm long, 1 cm wide
Real life: 10 m long, 5 m wide

Diagram: 3 cm long, 1 cm wide
Real life: 15 m long, 5 m wide

Two Steps to Construct Scale Drawings

1. **Divide** lengths by scale factor to get scale drawing lengths.
2. **Draw** the diagram using a **ruler**.

EXAMPLE

A rectangular allotment measuring 10 m by 6 m has been drawn using the scale 1 cm = 2 m. The allotment has a 3 m wide vegetable patch along the entire western edge, and a 2 m square shed in the north-east corner. Draw the vegetable patch and the shed on the scale drawing.

1. Vegetable patch
   Real life: 3 m wide
   Diagram: 1.5 cm wide

   Shed
   Real life: 2 m long, 2 m wide
   Diagram: 1 cm long, 1 cm wide

Section 3 — Ratio, Proportion and Rates of Change

Speed

Speed Formulas

SPEED — distance travelled per unit time.
Units of speed: e.g. km/h, m/s, mph
Use a **formula triangle** to remember formulas.

To use a formula triangle, cover what you want and write what's left.

$$\text{SPEED} = \frac{\text{DISTANCE}}{\text{TIME}}$$

Triangle: D on top, S × T on bottom

$$\text{DISTANCE} = \text{SPEED} \times \text{TIME}$$

$$\text{TIME} = \frac{\text{DISTANCE}}{\text{SPEED}}$$

Four Steps for Speed Questions

1. Write down the **formula triangle**.
2. Find the **formula**.
3. Put in the **numbers** (convert to the correct units if needed).
4. Add the **units**.

EXAMPLE

Kwame walks 7 miles in 2 hours. What is his average speed?

1. (triangle, cover S)
2. $\text{speed} = \dfrac{\text{distance}}{\text{time}} = \dfrac{7 \text{ miles}}{2 \text{ hours}}$
3.
4. $= 3.5$ mph

Distance is in miles and time is in hours so speed will be in miles per hour.

EXAMPLE

Dora kayaks across a lake. She travels at an average speed of 3 mph. It takes her 1 hour 45 minutes. How far does she kayak?

1. (triangle S × T)
2. distance = speed × time
3. Convert the time to hours:
   1 hour 45 mins = 1.75 hours
   So distance = 3 mph × 1.75 hours
4. $= 5.25$ miles

EXAMPLE

A cheetah runs 105 m at an average speed of 21 m/s. How long does it run for?

1. (triangle, cover T)
2. $\text{time} = \dfrac{\text{distance}}{\text{speed}}$
3. $= \dfrac{105 \text{ m}}{21 \text{ m/s}}$
4. $= 5$ seconds

Section 3 — Ratio, Proportion and Rates of Change

Section 4 — Geometry and Measures

Symmetry and Regular Polygons

Line Symmetry

LINE SYMMETRY — where the two parts of a shape on either side of a mirror line fold exactly together.

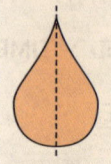

1 line of symmetry

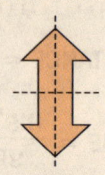

2 lines of symmetry

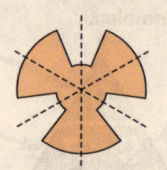

3 lines of symmetry

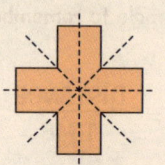

4 lines of symmetry

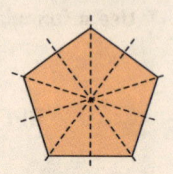

5 lines of symmetry

Rotational Symmetry

ROTATIONAL SYMMETRY — where a shape looks exactly the same after you rotate it into different positions.

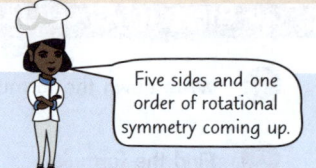

ORDER OF ROTATIONAL SYMMETRY — how many different positions look the same.

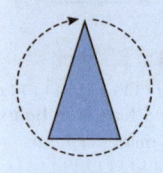

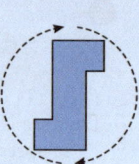

Order 1 — Same as no rotational symmetry.

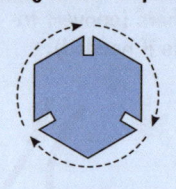

Order 2

Order 3

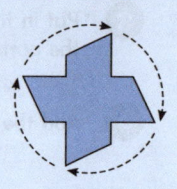

Order 4

Five sides and one order of rotational symmetry coming up.

Regular Polygons

Equilateral triangles and squares are regular polygons.

REGULAR POLYGON — all sides and angles are the same.

Name	Pentagon	Hexagon	Heptagon	Octagon	Nonagon	Decagon
No. of sides	5	6	7	8	9	10

Regular polygons have the same number of lines of symmetry as the number of sides. Their order of rotational symmetry is also the same.

Section 4 — Geometry and Measures

Triangles and Quadrilaterals

Four Types of Triangles

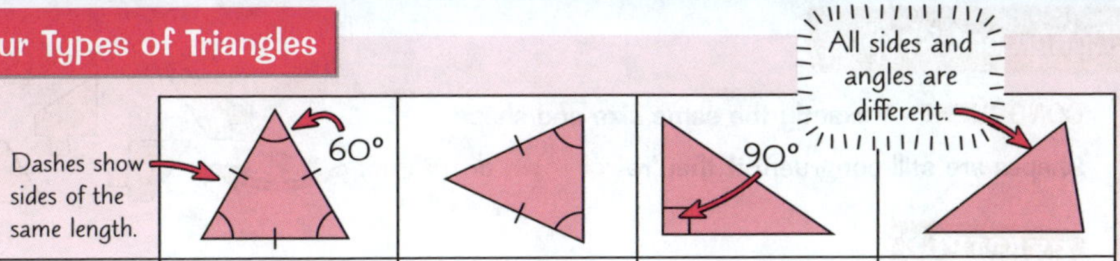

Dashes show sides of the same length.

All sides and angles are different.

Type	Equilateral	Isosceles	Right-angled	Scalene
Lines of symmetry	3	1	0 (unless isosceles)	0
Rotational symmetry	Order 3	None	None	None

Six Types of Quadrilaterals

SQUARE
- 4 equal angles of 90°
- 4 lines of symmetry
- Rotational symmetry order 4
- Diagonals cross at right angles

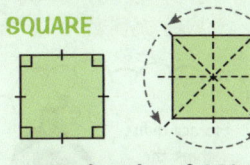

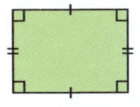

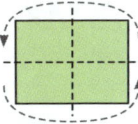

RECTANGLE
- 4 equal angles of 90°
- 2 lines of symmetry
- Rotational symmetry order 2

RHOMBUS

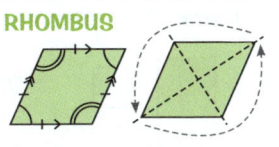

Arrows show that sides are parallel. Arcs show that angles are equal.

- 4 equal sides (opposites are parallel)
- 2 pairs of equal angles
- 2 lines of symmetry
- Rotational symmetry order 2
- Diagonals cross at right angles

PARALLELOGRAM
- 2 pairs of equal sides (sides in each pair are parallel)
- 2 pairs of equal angles
- No lines of symmetry
- Rotational symmetry order 2

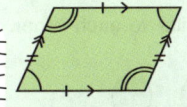

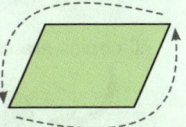

TRAPEZIUM
- 1 pair of parallel sides
- No lines of symmetry (unless isosceles)
- No rotational symmetry

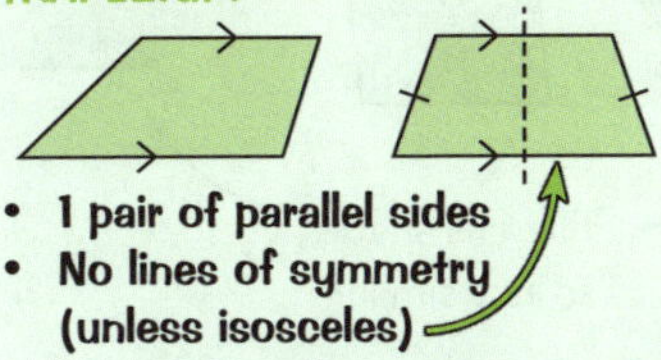

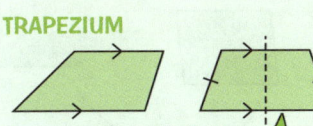

KITE
- 2 pairs of equal sides 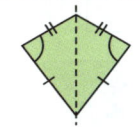
- 1 pair of equal angles
- 1 line of symmetry
- No rotational symmetry
- Diagonals cross at right angles.

Section 4 — Geometry and Measures

Congruence and Similarity

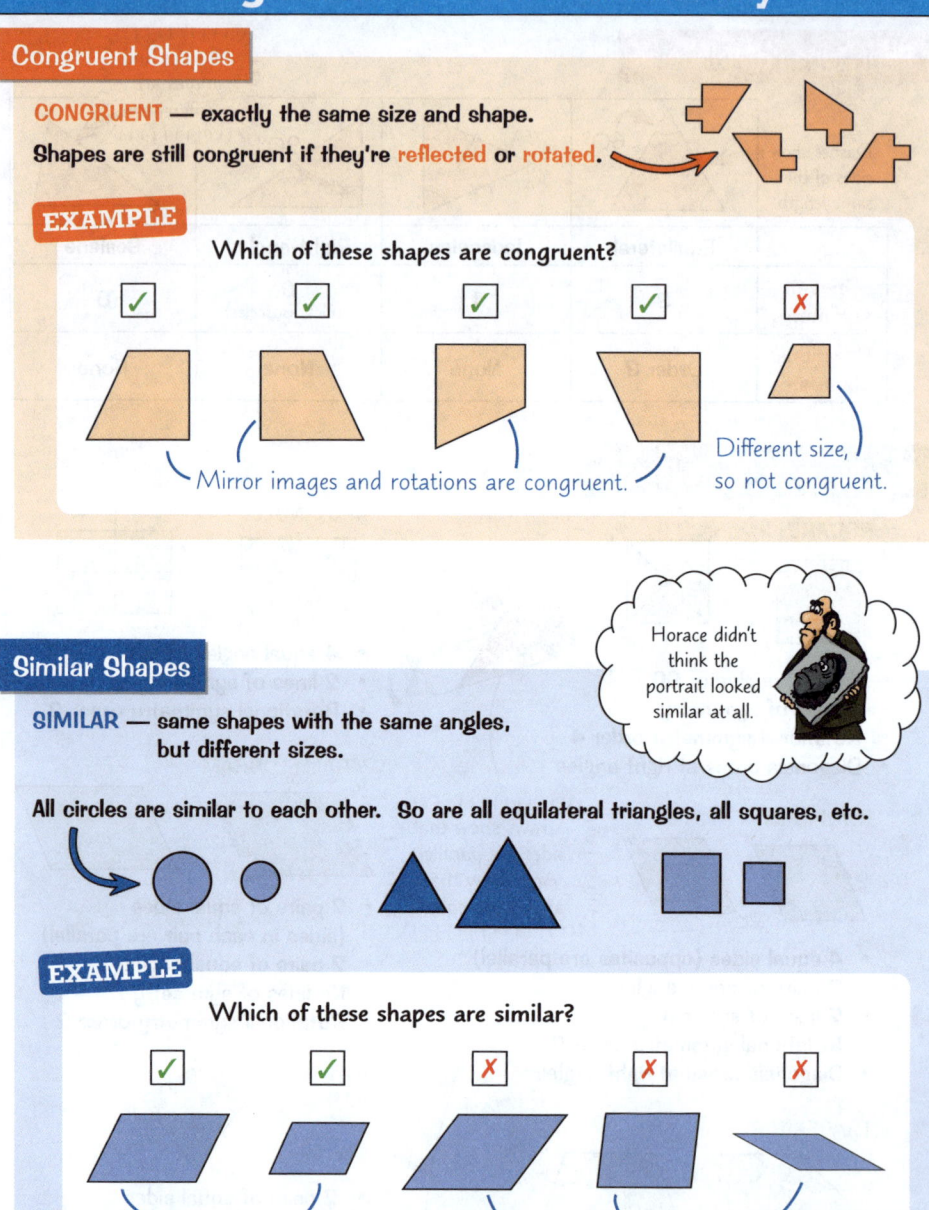

Congruent Shapes

CONGRUENT — exactly the same size and shape.
Shapes are still congruent if they're reflected or rotated.

EXAMPLE

Which of these shapes are congruent?

✓ ✓ ✓ ✓ ✗

Mirror images and rotations are congruent.

Different size, so not congruent.

Similar Shapes

SIMILAR — same shapes with the same angles, but different sizes.

All circles are similar to each other. So are all equilateral triangles, all squares, etc.

Horace didn't think the portrait looked similar at all.

EXAMPLE

Which of these shapes are similar?

✓ ✓ ✗ ✗ ✗

Same shape but different sizes, so similar.

Different shapes, so not similar.

Section 4 — Geometry and Measures

Perimeter and Area

Perimeter

PERIMETER — distance around the outside of a shape.

1. Put a blob on one corner of the shape.
2. Work out any missing lengths.
3. Write down the length of each side, starting from the blob.
4. Stop when you get back to the blob.
5. Add up all the side lengths.

EXAMPLE

Find the perimeter of this shape.

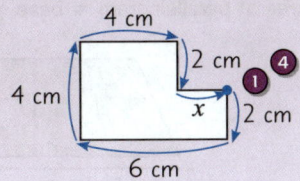

2. Missing length = x
   $x + 4$ cm = 6 cm
   So $x = 6 - 4 = 2$ cm

3. Lengths: 2 cm, 6 cm, 4 cm, 4 cm, 2 cm, 2 cm

5. Perimeter = 2 + 6 + 4 + 4 + 2 + 2 = 20 cm

Area of a Rectangle

AREA — space taken up by a shape.

Area of rectangle = length × width

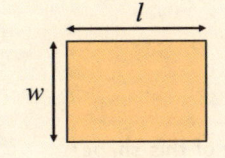

Squares have equal length and width so area = length².

EXAMPLE

Find the area of this rectangle.

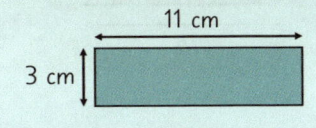

Area = 11 × 3 = 33 cm²

Area of a Triangle

Area of triangle = $\frac{1}{2}$ × base × vertical height

h_v is vertical height

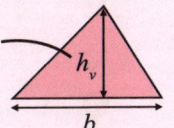

EXAMPLE

Find the area of this triangle.

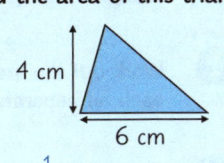

Area = $\frac{1}{2}$ × 6 × 4 = 12 cm²

Section 4 — Geometry and Measures

Area and Compound Area

Area of a Parallelogram

Area of parallelogram = base × vertical height

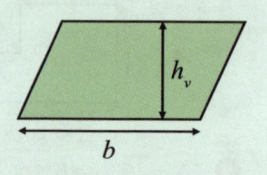

EXAMPLE

Find the area of this parallelogram.

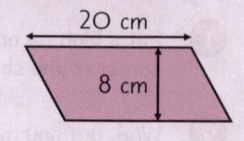

Area = 20 × 8 = 160 cm^2

Area of a Trapezium

Area of trapezium = $\frac{1}{2}$(a + b) × vertical height

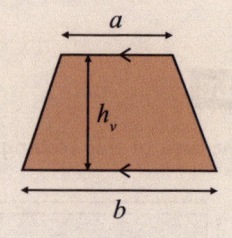

a and *b* are the parallel sides.

EXAMPLE

Find the area of this trapezium.

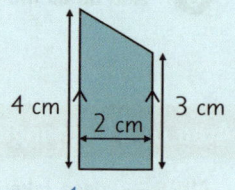

Area = $\frac{1}{2}$ × (4 + 3) × 2
= 7 cm^2

Areas of Compound Shapes

COMPOUND SHAPE — a shape that can be split up into other simpler shapes.

1. Split compound shapes into triangles and quadrilaterals.
2. Work out the area of each bit separately.
3. Add all of the areas together.

EXAMPLE

Find the area of this shape.

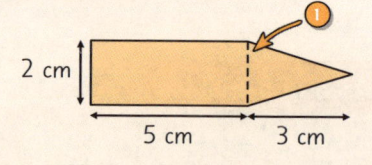

② Rectangle area = 5 × 2 = 10 cm^2
Triangle area = $\frac{1}{2}$ × 2 × 3 = 3 cm^2

③ Total area = 10 + 3 = 13 cm^2

Section 4 — Geometry and Measures

Circles

Radius and Diameter

DIAMETER — straight line across the circle that goes through its centre.

RADIUS — straight line from the centre of the circle to any point on the edge.

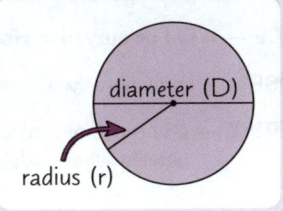

The radius is half the diameter.

Area

Area of a circle = $\pi \times$ (radius)^2
= πr^2

$\pi = 3.141592... \approx 3.142$

EXAMPLE
Find the area of a circle with a radius of 2 cm.
Area = $\pi \times 2^2$
= 12.566... cm^2
= 12.57 cm^2 (2 d.p.)

EXAMPLE
Isha bakes a pie with a diameter of 26 cm. She gives away three-quarters of the pie. Find the area of the remaining pie.

Radius = 26 ÷ 2 = 13 cm

Area of the whole pie = $\pi \times 13^2$
= 530.929... cm^2

Area of remaining pie = 530.929... ÷ 4
= 132.732... cm^2
= 132.73 cm^2 (2 d.p.)

Circumference

CIRCUMFERENCE — distance around the outside of the circle (its perimeter).

Circumference = $\pi \times$ diameter
= πD

OR

Circumference = $2 \times \pi \times$ radius
= $2\pi r$

EXAMPLE
A wheel has a diameter of 6 cm. What is its circumference?
Circumference = $\pi \times 6$
= 18.85 cm (2 d.p.)

EXAMPLE
Find the circumference of a circle with radius 4 cm.
Circumference = $2 \times \pi \times 4$
= 25.13 cm (2 d.p.)

Section 4 — Geometry and Measures

3D Shapes

Faces, Edges and Vertices

FACE — a flat or curved surface of a 3D shape.

EDGE — a line where two faces meet.

VERTEX — a corner point of a 3D shape, usually where edges meet.

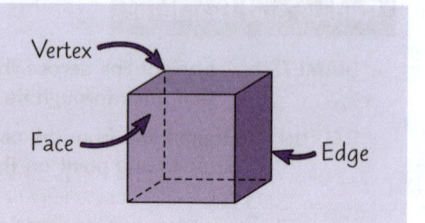

Cubes and Cuboids

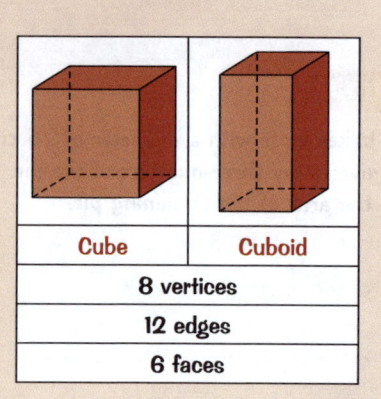

Cube	Cuboid
8 vertices	
12 edges	
6 faces	

Pyramids

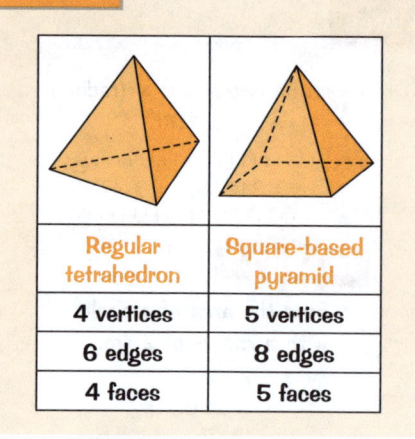

Regular tetrahedron	Square-based pyramid
4 vertices	5 vertices
6 edges	8 edges
4 faces	5 faces

Prisms and Cylinders

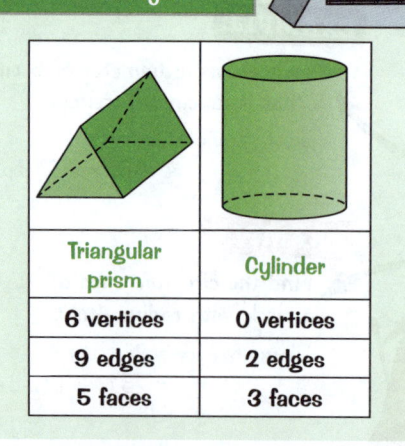

Triangular prism	Cylinder
6 vertices	0 vertices
9 edges	2 edges
5 faces	3 faces

Cones and Spheres

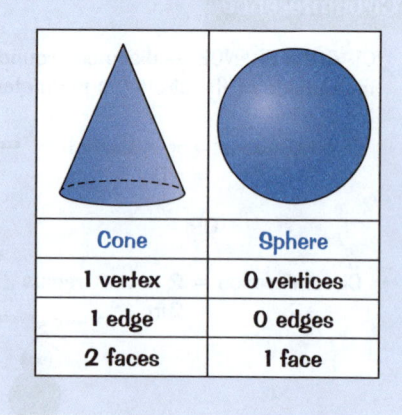

Cone	Sphere
1 vertex	0 vertices
1 edge	0 edges
2 faces	1 face

Section 4 — Geometry and Measures

Nets and Surface Area

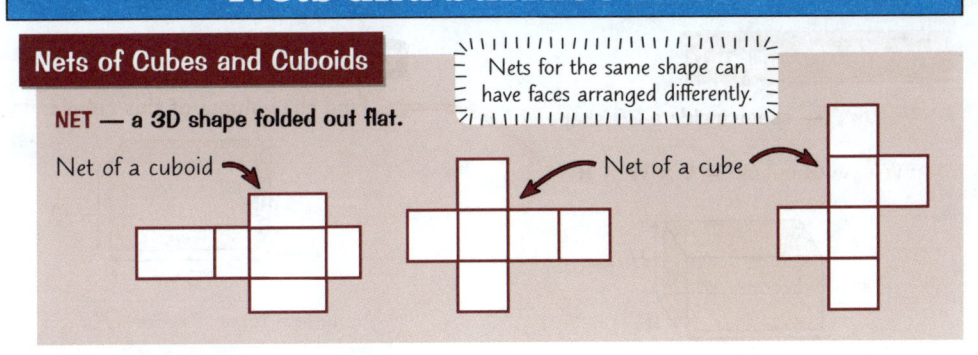

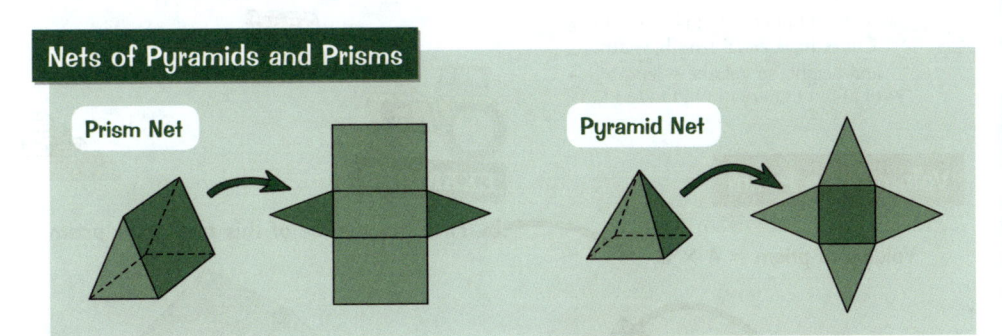

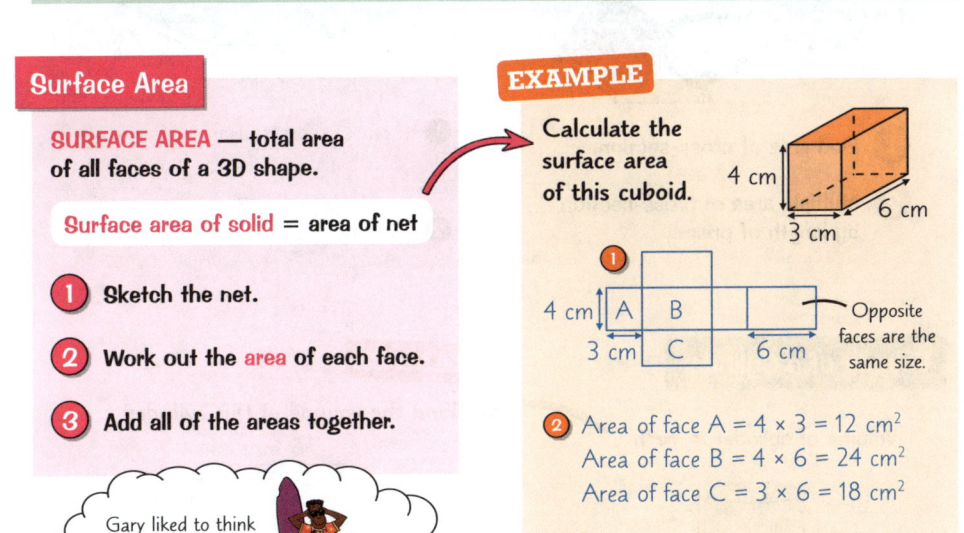

Nets of Cubes and Cuboids

NET — a 3D shape folded out flat.

Nets for the same shape can have faces arranged differently.

Net of a cuboid

Net of a cube

Nets of Pyramids and Prisms

Prism Net

Pyramid Net

Surface Area

SURFACE AREA — total area of all faces of a 3D shape.

Surface area of solid = area of net

1. Sketch the net.
2. Work out the area of each face.
3. Add all of the areas together.

Gary liked to think that the beach was a surfer's area.

EXAMPLE

Calculate the surface area of this cuboid.

4 cm, 6 cm, 3 cm

1. 4 cm | A | B | | |
   3 cm | C | | 6 cm

   Opposite faces are the same size.

2. Area of face A = 4 × 3 = 12 cm^2
   Area of face B = 4 × 6 = 24 cm^2
   Area of face C = 3 × 6 = 18 cm^2

3. Surface area = (2 × 12) + (2 × 24) + (2 × 18)
   = 108 cm^2

Section 4 — Geometry and Measures

Volume

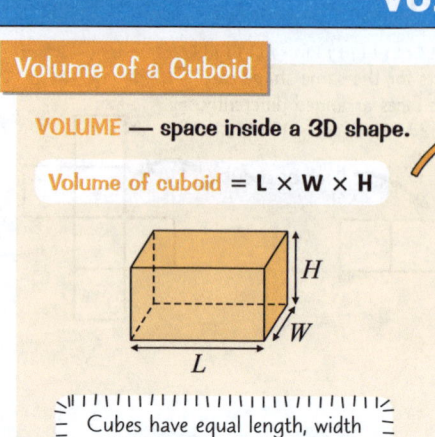

Volume of a Cuboid

VOLUME — space inside a 3D shape.

Volume of cuboid = L × W × H

Cubes have equal length, width and height, so volume = length³.

EXAMPLE
Find the volume of this cuboid.

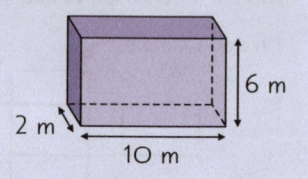

Volume = 10 × 2 × 6 = **120 m³**

Volume of a Prism

Volume of prism = A × L

A = constant area of cross-section

1. Find area of cross-section.
2. Multiply area of cross-section by length of prism.

EXAMPLE
Find the volume of this triangular prism.

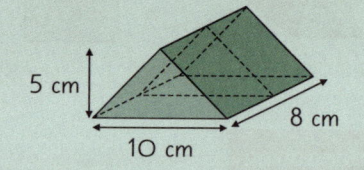

1. Area of cross-section = $\frac{1}{2}$ × 10 × 5
   = 25 cm²
2. Volume = 25 × 8 = **200 cm³**

Volume of a Cylinder

Volume of cylinder = πr²h

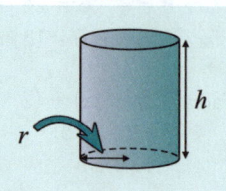

EXAMPLE
Find the volume of this cylinder.

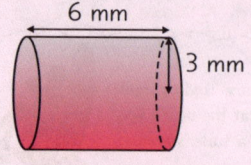

6 mm
3 mm

Volume = π × 3² × 6 = **169.65 mm³** (2 d.p.)

Section 4 — Geometry and Measures

Angle Basics

Four Special Angles

1) ONE-QUARTER TURN — 90°

2) HALF TURN (a straight line) — 180°

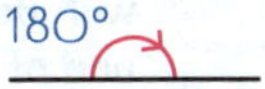

3) THREE-QUARTER TURN — 270°

4) FULL TURN — 360°

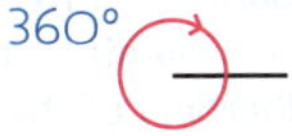

Angle Names

ACUTE angles — less than 90°

RIGHT angles — exactly 90°

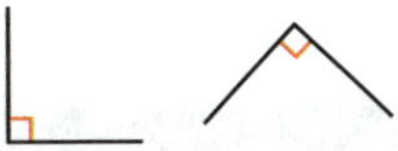

OBTUSE angles — between 90° and 180°

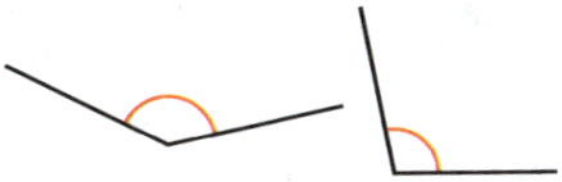

REFLEX angles — more than 180°

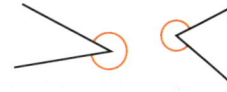

Jim had really good reflexes.

Three-Letter Angle Notation

Angles can be identified using **three letters** — the **middle** letter is the point where the angle is.

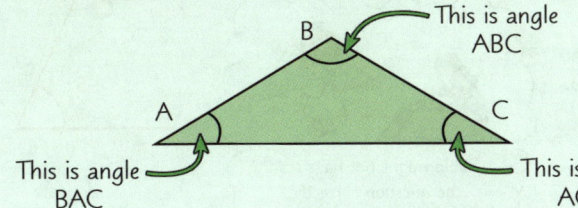

This is angle ABC

The other two letters tell you which two lines enclose the angle.

This is angle BAC

This is angle ACB

Section 4 — Geometry and Measures

Measuring and Drawing Angles

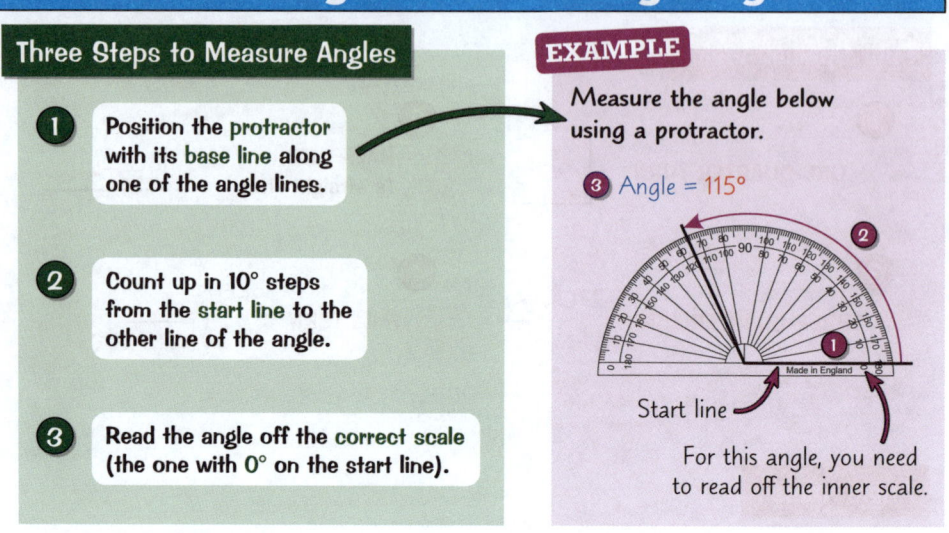

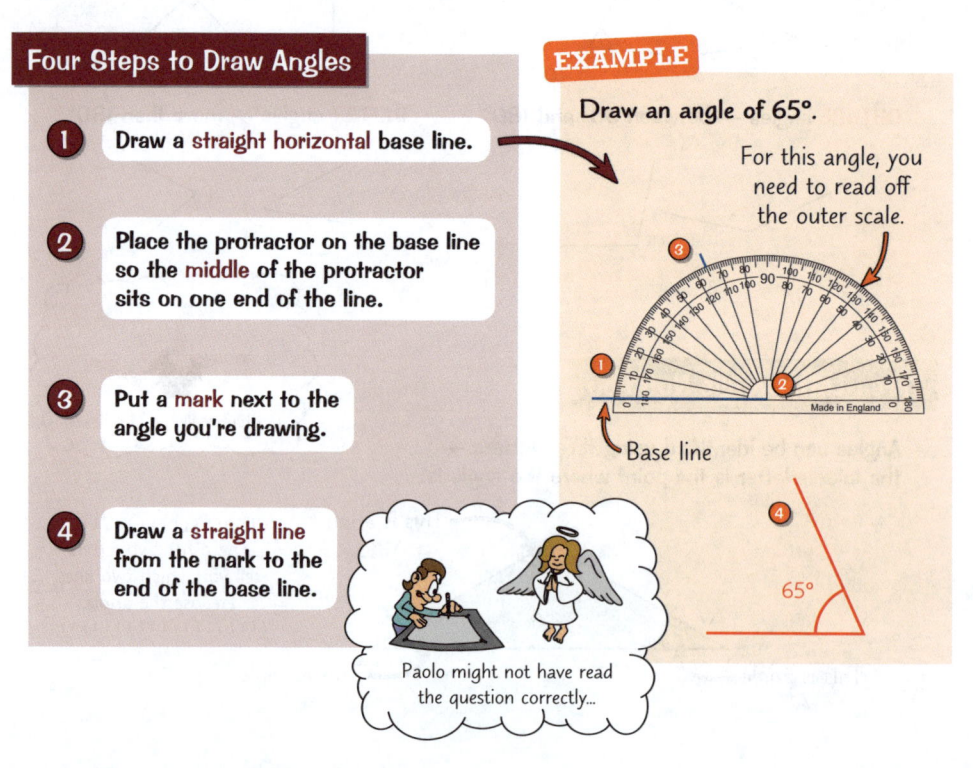

Three Steps to Measure Angles

1. Position the protractor with its base line along one of the angle lines.
2. Count up in 10° steps from the start line to the other line of the angle.
3. Read the angle off the correct scale (the one with 0° on the start line).

EXAMPLE

Measure the angle below using a protractor.

③ Angle = 115°

Start line

For this angle, you need to read off the inner scale.

Four Steps to Draw Angles

1. Draw a straight horizontal base line.
2. Place the protractor on the base line so the middle of the protractor sits on one end of the line.
3. Put a mark next to the angle you're drawing.
4. Draw a straight line from the mark to the end of the base line.

EXAMPLE

Draw an angle of 65°.

For this angle, you need to read off the outer scale.

Base line

65°

Paolo might not have read the question correctly...

Section 4 — Geometry and Measures

Geometry Rules

Five Angle Rules

1 Angles in a triangle add up to 180°.

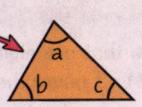

$a + b + c = 180°$

2 Angles on a straight line add up to 180°.

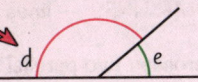

$d + e = 180°$

3 Angles in a quadrilateral add up to 360°.

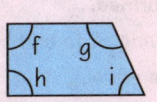

$f + g + h + i = 360°$

4 Angles round a point add up to 360°.

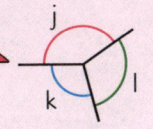

$j + k + l = 360°$

5 Isosceles triangles have 2 identical sides and 2 identical angles.

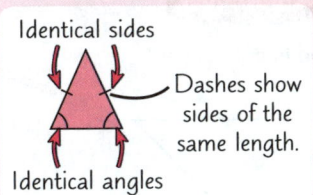

Identical sides
Dashes show sides of the same length.
Identical angles

GEOMETRY RULES!

Using Angle Rules

EXAMPLE

Find the sizes of angles x and y.

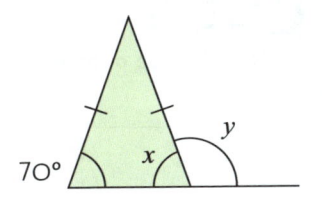

70°, x, y

Triangle is isosceles, so $x = 70°$

Angles on a straight line = 180°, so $y = 180° − 70° = 110°$

EXAMPLE

Find the sizes of angles a and b.

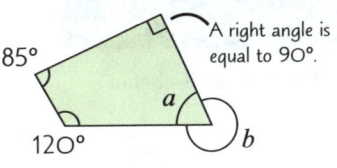

85°, 120°, a, b

A right angle is equal to 90°.

Angles in a quadrilateral = 360°
So $a = 360° − 90° − 85° − 120°$
     $= 65°$

Angles round a point = 360°
So $b = 360° − 65° = 295°$

Section 4 — Geometry and Measures

Parallel Lines

Parallel and Perpendicular Lines

PARALLEL LINES — lines that are always the same distance apart and never meet.

PERPENDICULAR LINES — lines that meet at a right angle.

When a line crosses two parallel lines:
- Two bunches of angles are formed.
- There are only two different angles (a and b).
- Vertically opposite angles are equal.

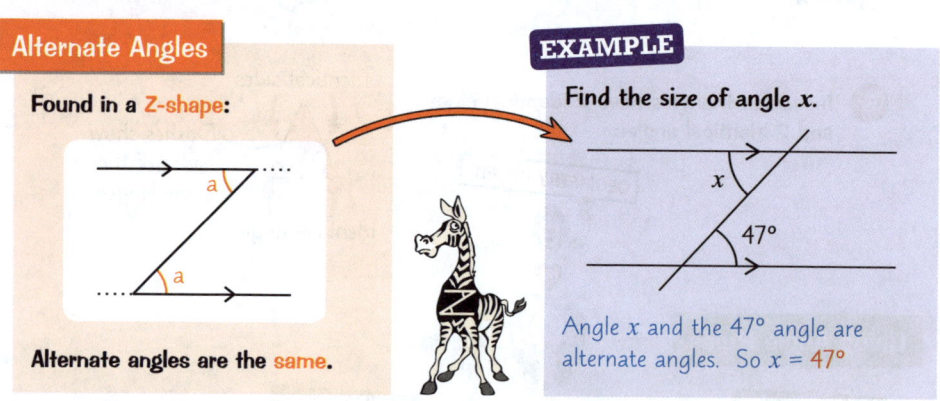

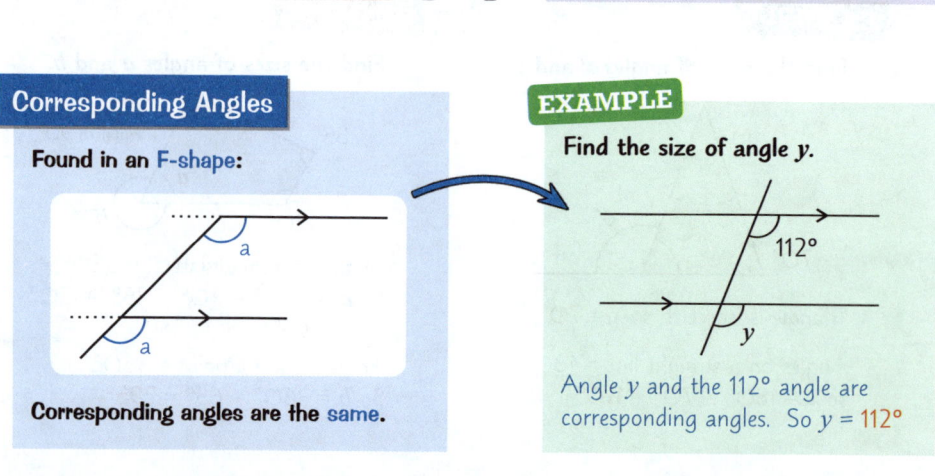

Arrows show that lines are parallel.

Alternate Angles

Found in a Z-shape:

Alternate angles are the same.

EXAMPLE

Find the size of angle x.

Angle x and the 47° angle are alternate angles. So $x = 47°$

Corresponding Angles

Found in an F-shape:

Corresponding angles are the same.

EXAMPLE

Find the size of angle y.

Angle y and the 112° angle are corresponding angles. So $y = 112°$

Section 4 — Geometry and Measures

Interior and Exterior Angles

For Any Polygon

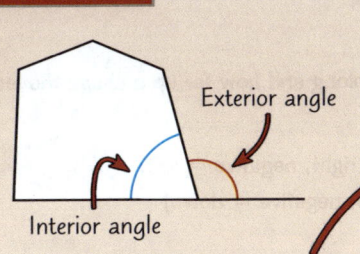

Sum of exterior angles = 360°

Interior angle = 180° − exterior angle

EXAMPLE

Find the size of angles x and y.

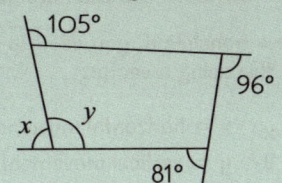

Sum of exterior angles = 360°
So $x = 360° − 105° − 96° − 81° = 78°$

Interior angle = 180° − exterior angle
So $y = 180° − 78° = 102°$

For Regular Polygons

Exterior angle = $\dfrac{360°}{n}$

n = number of sides

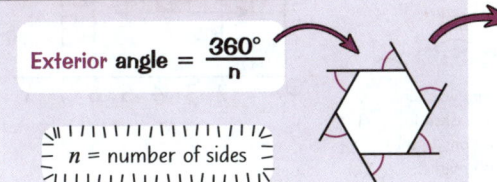

EXAMPLE

Find the size of an exterior angle of a regular pentagon.

A pentagon has 5 sides.
So exterior angle = $\dfrac{360°}{n} = \dfrac{360°}{5}$
$= 72°$

Sum of Interior Angles

For all polygons: Sum of interior angles = $(n − 2) \times 180°$

Hamish loved a spot of interior angling.

EXAMPLE

Find the value of x in the diagram.

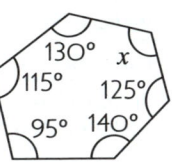

Find the sum of interior angles in a hexagon:
Sum of interior angles = $(n − 2) \times 180°$
$= (6 − 2) \times 180° = 720°$

Write as an equation and solve for x:
$x + 130° + 115° + 95° + 140° + 125° = 720°$
So $x = 720° − 130° − 115° − 95° − 140° − 125° = 115°$

Section 4 — Geometry and Measures

Translation and Reflection

Translation

TRANSLATION — a slide around a grid.

For a translation, you need to know how far along and how far up a shape moves. Do this using a **vector**:

$\begin{pmatrix} x \\ y \end{pmatrix}$ x = **horizontal** movement (positive = right, negative = left)
       y = **vertical** movement (positive = up, negative = down)

EXAMPLE

a) Translate shape A by the vector $\begin{pmatrix} -2 \\ 2 \end{pmatrix}$. Label the translated shape B.

This is a translation of 2 units left and 2 units up.

b) Describe the transformation that maps shape A onto shape C.

The shape moves 3 units right and 1 unit down. So it's a translation by the vector $\begin{pmatrix} 3 \\ -1 \end{pmatrix}$.

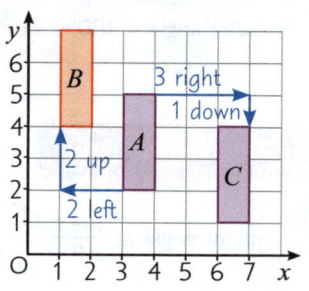

Moira was sure she'd asked for directions to the fish market...

Reflection

For a **reflection**, you need to know the **equation of the mirror line**:

x = 0	y-axis
y = 0	x-axis
x = a	vertical line
y = b	horizontal line
y = x	diagonal line from bottom left to top right
y = −x	diagonal line from top left to bottom right

Matching corners are the same distance from the mirror line.

EXAMPLE

a) Describe the transformation that maps shape A onto shape B.

B is a reflection of A in $y = x$

b) Reflect shape B in the mirror line $y = -1$. Label the new shape C.

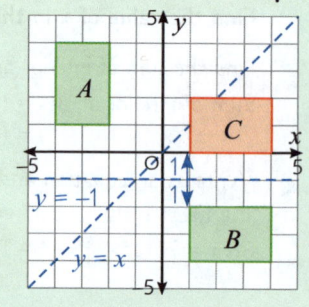

Section 4 — Geometry and Measures

Rotation and Enlargement

Rotation

For a rotation, you need to know:

1. the angle of rotation (90°, 180° or 270°)
2. the direction of rotation
   (clockwise or anticlockwise)
   The direction doesn't matter for a 180° rotation.
3. the centre of rotation
   To find this, trace the shape and rotate it around different points until it ends up on the image.

EXAMPLE

Describe the transformation that maps shape *A* onto shape *B*.

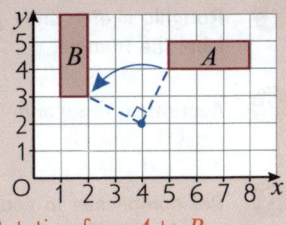

Rotation from *A* to *B*:
90° anticlockwise about (4, 2)

Enlargement

For an enlargement, you need to know the scale factor and the centre of enlargement.

$$\text{scale factor} = \frac{\text{new length}}{\text{old length}}$$

To find the centre of enlargement, draw lines through matching corners of the shapes and extend them until they cross.

Two steps to enlarge a shape:

1. Multiply side lengths by scale factor to find new side lengths.
2. Draw lines from centre of enlargement to shape, then extend by scale factor to find new position.

EXAMPLE

Enlarge shape *A* by a scale factor of 2 with centre of enlargement (1, 1). Label the new shape *B*.

1. Shape *A* is 2 units long and 1 unit wide. So shape *B* will be 2 × 2 = 4 units long and 1 × 2 = 2 units wide.
2. Draw lines, extend until they're twice as long, then join up to draw shape *B*.

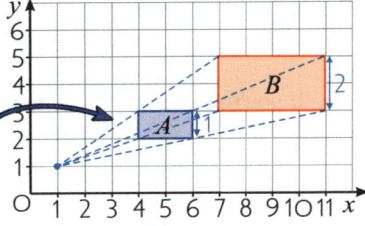

Section 4 — Geometry and Measures

Triangle Construction

Triangles — Three Known Sides

You need a **ruler** and a pair of **compasses**.

1. Roughly **sketch** and label the triangle.
2. Accurately draw and label the **base line**.
3. Set compasses to each side length, then draw an **arc** at each end.
4. **Join up** the ends of the base line with the point where the arcs cross. Label points and sides.

Leave your construction lines (e.g. compass marks) showing — don't rub them out.

EXAMPLE

Construct triangle ABC where AB = 4 cm, BC = 2 cm, AC = 3 cm.

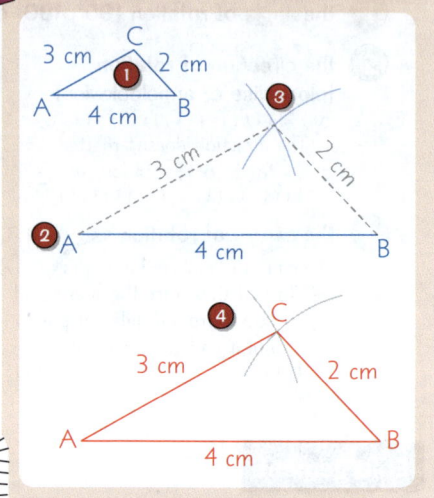

Triangles — Known Sides and Angles

You need a **ruler** and a **protractor**.

1. Roughly **sketch** and label the triangle.
2. Accurately draw and label the **base line**.
3. Use a **protractor** to measure any angles and mark out with dots.
4. If you're given **two angles**, draw lines from the ends of the base line through the dots. Label the intersection.

   If you're given **two sides**, measure towards the dot and label the point.
5. **Join up** the points. Label known sides and angles.

EXAMPLE

Construct triangle XYZ where XY = 3 cm, angle YXZ = 60°, angle XYZ = 30°.

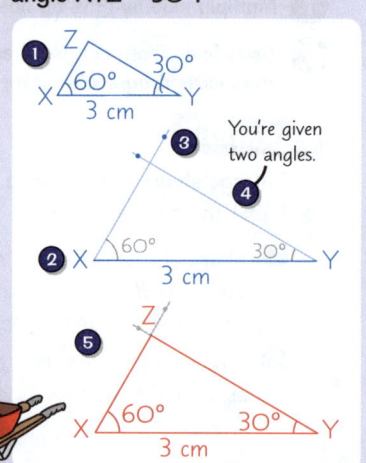

You're given two angles.

Section 4 — Geometry and Measures

Constructions

Perpendicular Bisector of a Line

PERPENDICULAR BISECTOR (of line segment AB) — a line at right angles to AB that passes through its midpoint.

1 Put compass point on **A** and draw **two arcs** either side of it.

2 Repeat for point **B**, making sure the arcs **cross**. Keep the compass settings the **same**.

3 **Join** the two points where the arcs cross with a straight line.

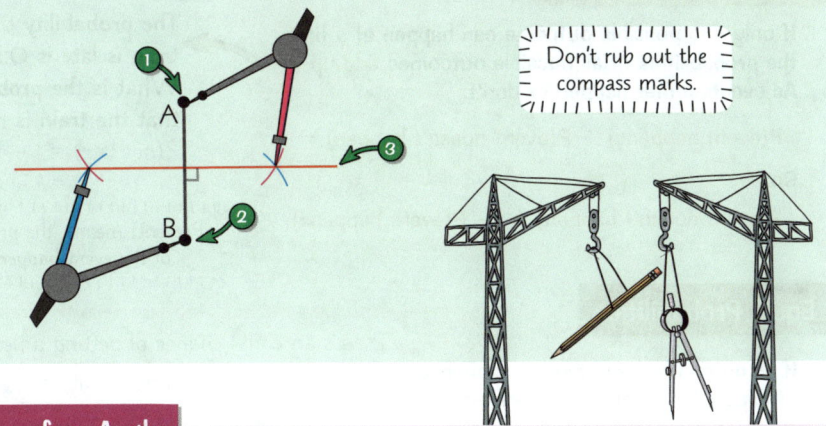

Don't rub out the compass marks.

Bisector of an Angle

BISECTOR OF AN ANGLE — a line that divides an angle exactly in half.

1 Put the compass point on point of angle and draw an **arc** on each line.

2 Keeping the compass setting the **same**, draw **another arc** from each of the first arcs.

3 **Join** the point where the arcs cross to the point of the angle with a straight line.

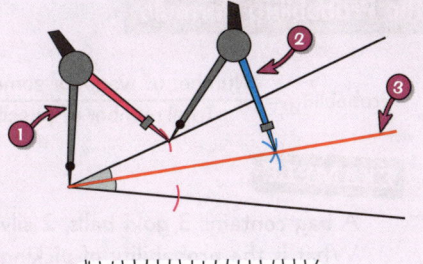

The construction forms two equal angles.

Section 4 — Geometry and Measures

Probability

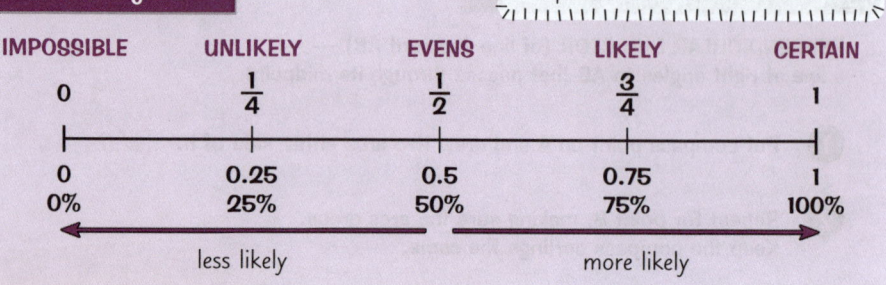

The Probability Scale

All probabilities are between 0 and 1.

IMPOSSIBLE	UNLIKELY	EVENS	LIKELY	CERTAIN
0	$\frac{1}{4}$	$\frac{1}{2}$	$\frac{3}{4}$	1
0	0.25	0.5	0.75	1
0%	25%	50%	75%	100%

← less likely   more likely →

Probabilities of Events

If only **one** possible outcome can happen at a time, the probabilities of all possible outcomes **add up to 1**. As events either happen or don't:

P(event happens) + P(event doesn't happen) = 1

So:

P(event doesn't happen) = 1 − P(event happens)

EXAMPLE

The probability that a train is late is 0.2. What is the probability that the train is not late?

P(not late) = 1 − P(late)
= 1 − 0.2 = 0.8

P(event) means "the probability of the event happening".

Equal Probabilities

If all outcomes have the **same** chance of happening, probabilities are **equal**. The probabilities depend on the number of **possible outcomes**.

There's an equal chance of getting a head or tail when you toss a coin (probability = $\frac{1}{2}$).

There's an equal chance of getting any of the six numbers when you roll a dice (probability = $\frac{1}{6}$).

The Probability Formula

$$\text{Probability} = \frac{\text{Number of ways for something to happen}}{\text{Total number of possible outcomes}}$$

You can only use this formula if all the outcomes are equally likely — e.g. for a fair coin, dice or spinner.

EXAMPLE

A bag contains 3 gold balls, 2 silver balls and 5 black balls. What is the probability of picking a silver ball at random?

$$\text{Probability} = \frac{\text{number of silver balls}}{\text{total number of balls}} = \frac{2}{10} = \frac{1}{5}$$

Simplify if you can.
There are 3 + 2 + 5 = 10 balls, so 10 possible outcomes.

Section 5 — Probability and Statistics

Listing Outcomes

Lists of Outcomes

For two simple things happening together, list all the possible outcomes. E.g.

Tossing two coins:
HH HT TH TT

Meal options (starter, main):
soup, chilli   soup, lasagne   melon, chilli   melon, lasagne

Work out probabilities from your list — put numbers into probability formula:

P(exactly one head) = $\frac{2}{4} = \frac{1}{2}$

2 outcomes have exactly one head
Count the total outcomes

Sample Space Diagrams

A two-way table that shows all possible outcomes for two things happening. Use them to find probabilities.

EXAMPLE

Draw a sample space diagram showing all possible outcomes when two fair spinners labelled A, B, C and 1, 2, 3 are spun. Use it to find the probability of spinning a B and an odd number.

Outcomes for 123 spinner

3 outcomes for each spinner, so 3 × 3 = 9 possible outcomes.

9 possible outcomes, 2 of them are B and odd, so P(B and odd) = $\frac{2}{9}$.

	A	B	C
1	A1	(B1)	C1
2	A2	B2	C2
3	A3	(B3)	C3

Outcomes for ABC spinner

Combining Outcomes

If all outcomes are numbers (e.g. two numbered spinners), you might have to combine the outcomes by adding, subtracting, multiplying or dividing.

EXAMPLE

Two spinners numbered 1-3 are spun and the scores are multiplied. Draw a sample space diagram and use it to find the probability of getting a result of 6 or more.

There are 9 possible outcomes and 3 of them are 6 or more, so P(6 or more) = $\frac{3}{9} = \frac{1}{3}$.

×	1	2	3
1	1	2	3
2	2	4	(6)
3	3	(6)	(9)

Section 5 — Probability and Statistics

Venn Diagrams

Sets

SET — a collection of elements (e.g. numbers), written in curly brackets { }.

ξ	the universal set (the group of things elements are selected from).
n(A)	the number of elements in set A.

EXAMPLE

ξ = numbers from 1-10 and set A = factors of 20. Write out the elements of each set and find n(A).

ξ = {1, 2, 3, 4, 5, 6, 7, 8, 9, 10}
A = {1, 2, 4, 5, 10}   n(A) = 5

20 is a factor of 20, but it's not in A as it's not in the universal set.

Sets and Venn Diagrams

VENN DIAGRAM — a diagram where sets are represented by overlapping circles. The rectangle represents the universal set.

INTERSECTION — overlap of circles. Elements that belong to both sets go here.

E.g. to show which pupils in a class play hockey (H) or badminton (B):

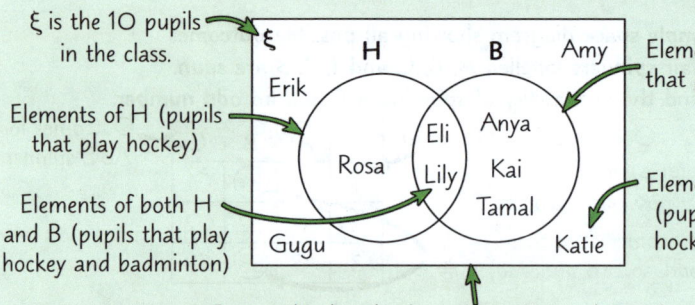

- ξ is the 10 pupils in the class.
- Elements of H (pupils that play hockey)
- Elements of both H and B (pupils that play hockey and badminton)
- Elements of B (pupils that play badminton)
- Elements not in H or B (pupils that don't play hockey or badminton)

H: Erik, Rosa, Gugu
H ∩ B: Eli, Lily
B: Anya, Kai, Tamal
Outside: Amy, Katie

Rosa only plays hockey. Anya, Kai and Tamal only play badminton. Eli and Lily play both sports. The rest play neither sport.

Number of Elements

Venn diagrams can also show the number of elements.
So for the Venn diagram above:

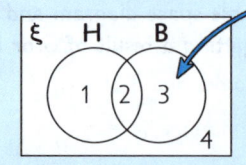

ξ | H: 1 | H∩B: 2 | B: 3 | outside: 4

e.g. n(B) = 2 + 3 = 5

Don't forget to include the elements in the overlap when finding the number of elements in a set

Section 5 — Probability and Statistics

Types of Data and Line Graphs

Types of Data

PRIMARY DATA	Data you've collected yourself.	Measuring the heights of your friends, recording colours of cars in a car park
SECONDARY DATA	Data collected by someone else.	Information from a census, survey results from the internet
QUALITATIVE DATA	Data described by words (not numbers).	Eye colour, favourite flavour of ice cream, make of a car
QUANTITATIVE DATA	Data described by numbers.	Height of a tree, time taken to get to school
DISCRETE DATA	Data that can only take exact values.	Number of siblings, number of goals scored in a match
CONTINUOUS DATA	Data that can take any value in a range.	Mass of a car, length of a pencil, reaction time

Line Graphs

LINE GRAPH — set of points joined with straight lines. Often has time on horizontal axis to show changes over time.

Sales increased sharply after the product was launched, then dropped off gradually.

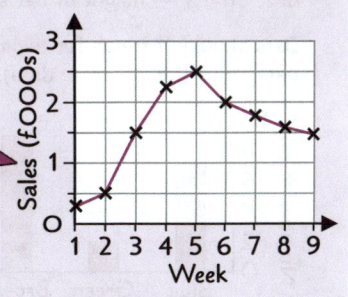

Draw two lines on the same graph to compare things.

The number of visitors to the ice rink decreased until August then increased.

The number of visitors to the theme park increased until August then decreased.

Leona was beginning to wish she'd chosen the ice rink...

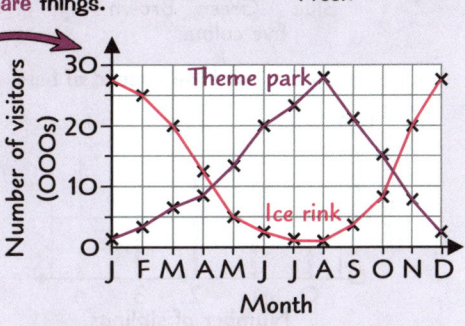

Section 5 — Probability and Statistics

Pictograms and Bar Charts

Pictograms

PICTOGRAM — uses symbols to show frequency.

Frequency means 'how many'.

The key shows what one symbol represents.
A fraction of a symbol represents that fraction of the frequency.

EXAMPLE

This pictogram shows the number of dogs in a park.

a) How many collies are there?
There are 2 whole symbols and 1 half symbol, so there are 2 + 2 + 1 = 5 collies.

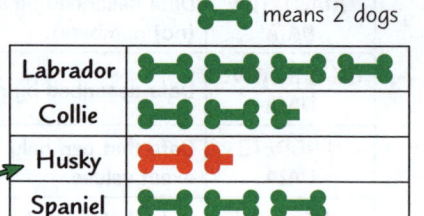

b) There are 3 huskies. Draw this on the pictogram.
3 dogs = 1 whole symbol and 1 half symbol

Key: 🦴 means 2 dogs

Labrador	🦴 🦴 🦴 🦴
Collie	🦴 🦴 ½
Husky	🦴 ½
Spaniel	🦴 🦴 🦴

Bar Charts

BAR CHART — height of bar shows frequency.

Bars shouldn't touch for separate categories (i.e. discrete data).

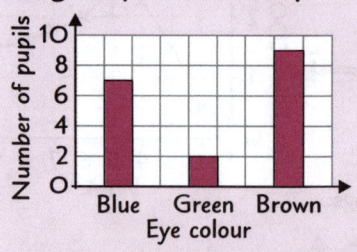

Bars should touch when there's a range of values on the x-axis (i.e. continuous data).

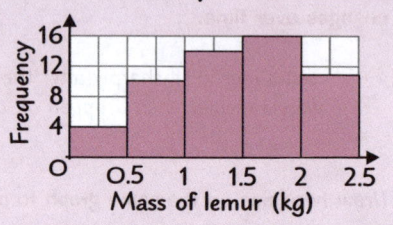

A bar-line graph has lines instead of bars.

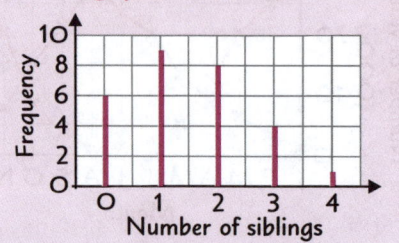

Use dual bar charts to compare data sets.

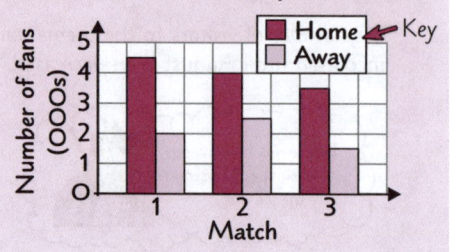

Key: Home / Away

Section 5 — Probability and Statistics

Pie Charts

Pie Charts and Proportion

Total of all data = 360°

Work out missing **angles** and **fractions** of the total using the information given.

This pie chart shows some people's favourite types of film.

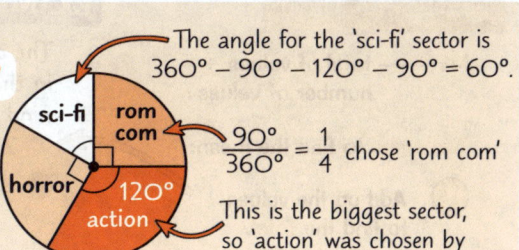

The angle for the 'sci-fi' sector is $360° - 90° - 120° - 90° = 60°$.

$\frac{90°}{360°} = \frac{1}{4}$ chose 'rom com'

This is the biggest sector, so 'action' was chosen by the most people.

Four Steps to Draw Pie Charts

1. Add up the numbers to find the **total**.
2. Divide 360° by the total to find the **multiplier**.
3. Multiply each number by the multiplier to find the **angle**.
4. Draw the pie chart accurately using a **protractor**.

EXAMPLE

1. Total = 35 + 40 + 15 = 90
2. Multiplier = 360° ÷ 90 = 4°

Music	Rock	Pop	Jazz
Number	35	40	15
Angle	140°	160°	60°

3. E.g. 35 × 4° = 140°

4. Check that the angles add up to 360°:
$140° + 160° + 60° = 360°$

Two Steps to Find How Many in a Category

1. Divide 360° by the total to find the angle for **one item**.
2. Divide the angle for a category by the angle for one item.

EXAMPLE

180 people were asked what their favourite season is. The results are shown in the pie chart. How many people said 'Summer'?

1. 360° ÷ 180 = 2° per person
2. 110° ÷ 2° = 55 people said 'Summer'

Section 5 — Probability and Statistics

Mean, Median, Mode and Range

Finding the Mean

MEAN — total of values ÷ number of values

Two steps to find the mean:

1. Add up the values to find the *total*.
2. Divide the total by the *number of values*.

EXAMPLE

The data below shows the number of pages in the 6 books Jiya has read so far this year. Find the mean for the data.

224   286   408   284   290   224

1. $224 + 286 + 408 + 284 + 290 + 224 = 1716$
2. Mean = $\frac{1716}{6}$ = 286 pages

Finding the Median

MEDIAN — middle value (when values are in size order)

Two steps to find the median:

1. Put the values in *order*.
2. For an *odd* number of values, the median is the *middle value*.

   For an *even* number of values, the median is *halfway* between the *two middle values*.

EXAMPLE

The data below shows the number of pupils on 6 different school buses. Find the median for the data.

18   27   36   14   25   33

1. In order:
   14   18   (25   27)   33   36
2. Median is halfway between 25 and 27, which is 26 pupils.

The mean, median and mode are all averages.

Finding the Mode and Range

MODE — most common value
Data sets can have *more than one* mode, or *no* mode at all.

RANGE — difference between highest and lowest values

Putting data in order of size helps when finding the mode and range too.

EXAMPLE

The data below shows the number of people in the audience at a theatre each night for a week. Find the mode and range for the data.

126   98   144   167   186   144   128

Mode = 144 people
Range = $186 - 98$ = 88 people

Section 5 — Probability and Statistics

Frequency Tables

Frequency Tables

FREQUENCY TABLE — shows how many things there are in each category.

This frequency table shows how many cars some families own.

Category

E.g. 7 families have 2 cars.

Number of cars	Tally	Frequency
0	IIII I	6
1	IIII IIII II	12
2	IIII II	7
3	III	3

Use a tally column to record results.

Count up the tallies to find frequencies.

A grouped frequency table puts data into classes that cover a range of values.

Number of rooms	1-10	11-20	21-30	31-40
Frequency	5	17	22	32

This grouped frequency table shows how many rooms some hotels have.

E.g. 22 hotels have between 21 and 30 rooms.

Four Steps to Find the Mean

1 Add up the numbers in the frequency column to find the **total frequency**.

Your table might have rows instead of columns — it works in just the same way.

2 **Multiply** each category by its frequency and put the results in a new column.

3 **Add** up the numbers in the new column.

4 **Divide** the new total by the total frequency to find the mean.

EXAMPLE

Number of pets	Frequency	Number of pets × Frequency
0	5	**2** 0 × 5 = 0
1	11	1 × 11 = 11
2	7	2 × 7 = 14
3	2	3 × 2 = 6
Total	**1** 25	**3** 31

Find the mean number of pets.

Total number of pets

4 Mean = $\frac{31}{25}$ = 1.24 pets

Total number of people asked

The mode is the category with the highest frequency — here it's 1.

Section 5 — Probability and Statistics

Scatter Graphs

Scatter Graphs and Correlation

SCATTER GRAPH — plots one thing against another.

CORRELATION — shows how closely the two things are related.

STRONG correlation	Two things are closely related. Points make a fairly straight line.
WEAK correlation	Two things are loosely related. Points don't line up quite as neatly.
NO correlation	Two things are unrelated. Points are scattered randomly.
POSITIVE correlation	Two things increase or decrease together. Points slope uphill from left to right.
NEGATIVE correlation	One thing increases as the other decreases. Points slope downhill from left to right.

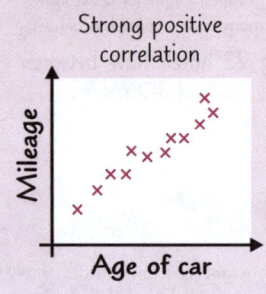

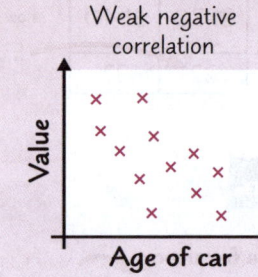

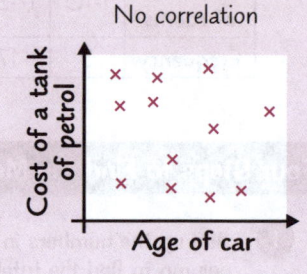

Strong positive correlation — Mileage vs Age of car

Weak negative correlation — Value vs Age of car

No correlation — Cost of a tank of petrol vs Age of car

Lines of Best Fit

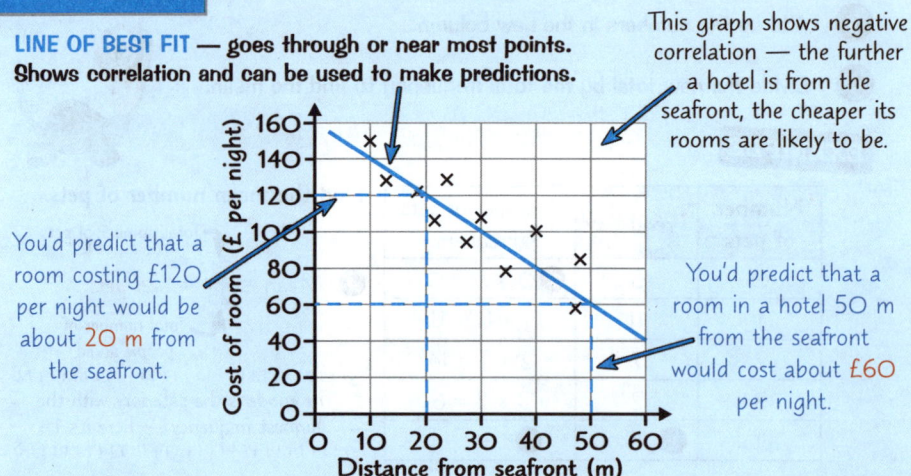

LINE OF BEST FIT — goes through or near most points. Shows correlation and can be used to make predictions.

This graph shows negative correlation — the further a hotel is from the seafront, the cheaper its rooms are likely to be.

You'd predict that a room costing £120 per night would be about 20 m from the seafront.

You'd predict that a room in a hotel 50 m from the seafront would cost about £60 per night.

Cost of room (£ per night) vs Distance from seafront (m)

Section 5 — Probability and Statistics